# FABULOUS
# POULTRY & GAME

by
## Johna Blinn

Edited by
**Tom Dorsey**

**PUBLISHED BY PLAYMORE INC., PUBLISHERS AND WALDMAN PUBLISHING CORP.**
New York, New York
**Printed in Canada / Cover Printed in the United States of America**

Fabulous Cookbook Series
Prepared Under the Editorial Direction of
Joshua Hanft

Illustrated by Arthur Friedman

Designed by Irva Mandelbaum

*Cover photo: Roast Chicken*
*Courtesy of National Broiler Council*

## Acknowledgments:

This writer is especially indebted to the expert advice, encouragement and cooperation of many. I am particularly indebted to Ruth Lundgren, Olive Dempsey, Chris Pines, Caryl Saunders, Claire Boasi, Anita Fial, Pat Mason, A.C. Collins, Marilyn Kaytor, Ed Justin, The Fresh Garlic Association, Lea & Perrins Worcestershire Sauce, American Mushroom Association, Tuna Research Foundation, McIlhenny Co., Anita Mizner, Howard Helmer, Prince Foods Light Pasta, Barbara Robinson, Sunkist Growers, Inc., California Milk Advisory Board, American Egg Board, Florida Celery Committee, California Iceberg Lettuce Commission, American Dairy Association, American Spice Trade Association, Virginia Schroeder, Alice Gautsch, Eileen Edwards Denne, Borden's Lite-Line Pasteurized Process Cheese Product, Quaker Oats Co., Carolyn Coughlin, California Fresh Market Tomato Advisory Board, Margaret Spader, Fleischmann's (unsalted margarine and 100% corn oil margarine), Florida Citrus Commission, National Broiler Council, Idaho Potato Commission, California Table Grape Commission, Campbell Soup Co., Angostura International Limited, Rice Council, Rae Hartfield, Betsy Slinkard, Argo and Kingsford's Corn Starch, United Fresh Fruit and Vegetable Association, Gloria Marshall, Marilyn Dompe, National Fisheries Institute, Inc., Patricia O'Keefe, California Artichoke Advisory Board, Mazola Corn Oil, Castle & Cooke Foods (Dole/Bumble Bee), Virginia Pinegreen, Donna Higgins, Del Monte Kitchens, Dot Tringali, Kay Murphy O'Flynn, Washington State Apple Commission, Dee Munson, Lois Westlund, Egg Beaters Cholesterol-free Egg Substitute, California Avocado Commission, Charcoal Briquet Institute, Alaska Seafood Marketing Institute, Washington State Potato Commission, Hellmann's and Best Foods Mayonnaise, Roxie Howlett, Diamond Walnut Kitchen, Skippy Peanut Butter, Karo Corn Syrup, Planter's Peanut Oil Test Kitchen, Standard Brands, Inc., National Turkey Federation, Christine Dozel, Jan Kerman, South African Rock Lobster Service Corporation, Nucoa Margarine, Diane Cline, Frances Fleming, Virginia Schroeder, Lawry's Ltd., California Milk Advisory Board, Ray Clark, National Duckling Council, California Bartlett Growers, Inc., O'Neal F. Caliendo, Yvonne Martin, National Capon Council, National Goose Council, National Livestock and Meat Board, American Lamb Council, Olive Administrative Committee, Fleischmann's Active Dry Yeast, Blue Bonnet Margarine, California Dried Fig Advisory Board, Beef Industry Council, Peanut Advisory Board, National Pork Producers Council, Kikkoman International Inc., New Zealand Lamb Co., Jan Works, Schiling Division McCormick and Co., National Cherry Growers & Industries Foundation, Susan Martinson, Jan Sirochman, Golden Grain Macaroni Co., Sweet Potato Council of California, Donna Hamilton, B.J. McCabe, Leafy Greens Council, Marcia L. Watts, California Turkey Industry Board, Frani Lauda, Italian Wine Center, National Macaroni Institute, J. Marsiglia, California Almond Growers Exchange, Bertolli's (olive oil, red-Italian wine vinegar, spaghetti sauce and wines), North American Blueberry Council, Fenella Pearson, Florio (dry and sweet Marsala wines), Ken Bray, 21 Brands (Liquore Galliano), Sherrie Newman, Wyler's Beef-Flavored Instant Bouillon, Jamaica Resort Hotels, Borden Company, Los Angeles Smoking and Curing Company, Mrs. Cubbison's Foods, Inc., Catherine Stratemeyer, Southern Belle English Walnuts, Denmark Cheese Association, Shirley Mack, Beans of the West, International Multifoods (Kretschmer Wheat Germ) and Imported Winter Grapes Association.

J.B.

BARONET
B·O·O·K·S

BARONET BOOKS is a trademark of Playmore Inc., Publishers
and Waldman Publishing Corp., New York, N.Y.

# The Author

To many of the top movie and television stars, Johna Blinn is a celebrity. For almost 20 years they have welcomed her into their homes, onto sets, just about anywhere to talk about food, entertaining and lifestyles. Her column, "Celebrity Cookbook," is syndicated throughout the world and appears weekly in more than 140 newspapers and periodicals. A collection of hundreds of these conversations and recipes appears in *Celebrity Cookbook*, published by Waldman Publishing Corporation.

Blinn is a former assistant food editor of LOOK magazine and is the author of a number of books, including *The Shangri-la Cookbook*. While she is busy working on her first novel and screenplay, Blinn still manages to serve as a frequent contributor of indepth interviews, profiles and entertainment features to newspapers and magazines in the U. S. and abroad.

A graduate of the State University of Iowa, Blinn took graduate work in home economics at the University of Wisconsin and taught home economics in Iowa, Virginia and New York. Now based in Los Angeles, she is married to a nationally-known newspaper syndicate editor, writer and management consultant, and they have two teenage children.

# CONTENTS

# Bagged Italian Rock Cornish Hens

Serves 4 to 6

1 package long grain and wild rice mix, or use your favorite stuffing
4 to 6 Rock Cornish hens, each weighing about 1 pound
8 cloves garlic, peeled and sliced
3 slices peeled ginger root, chopped
½ cup soy sauce
½ cup honey
1½ teaspoons salt
½ teaspoon paprika
about 2 cups all-purpose flour
1 large paper or plastic bag
4 to 6 small (lunch-size) brown paper bags
vegetable oil

1. Cook rice according to package directions. Allow to cool.
2. Wash hens and dry inside and out.
3. Cook garlic, ginger root, soy sauce, honey, salt and paprika, stirring until mixture comes to a boil. Remove from heat.
4. Put flour and hens into large paper bag; close and shake to coat with flour.
5. Roll floured hens in soy sauce mixture, or spoon sauce over hens to coat evenly.
6. Put small paper bags on cookie sheet. (Do one at a time.)
7. Pour vegetable oil over bag, saturating it well. (This is messy but necessary.) Wipe excess oil from cookie sheet.
8. Spoon stuffing into hens.
9. Slip each hen into oiled paper bag. Staple end shut.
10. Place bags of hens on racks on cookie sheet. Bake in preheated 350° F. oven 1 hour.
11. Split bags open. If not browned enough, return to oven for a few more minutes.

# Rock Cornish Hens Supreme

Serves 6

6 Rock Cornish hens
½ cup butter or margarine
1½ teaspoons garlic salt
1½ teaspoons parsley
1½ teaspoons salt
1 teaspoon rosemary, crumbled
¼ teaspoon white pepper
1 onion, peeled and minced
for garnish:
   parsley sprigs, lemon slices and seedless green grapes, cut in small bunches

1. Arrange cleaned hens in lightly greased shallow pan.
2. Melt butter in saucepan; add all remaining ingredients except onion and garnish. Mix well.
3. Brush mixture evenly on each hen; sprinkle onion over top.
4. Bake, uncovered, in preheated 400° F. oven 1 hour, basting often.
5. Serve on heated platter with parsley sprigs, lemon slices and grapes for garnish.

# Cornish Game Hens with Wheat Germ & Honey-Soy Sauce

Serves 4

4 Rock Cornish hens, thawed
salt
pepper
1 can (8¼ ounces) crushed
   pineapple
¾ cup regular wheat germ

⅓ cup green onion, minced
3 tablespoons melted butter
   or margarine
1 tablespoon soy sauce
⅛ teaspoon rosemary leaves,
   crushed

1. Wash hens in cold water; pat dry. Sprinkle cavities with salt and papper.
2. Drain pineapple, reserving 2 tablespoons syrup for Honey Soy Glaze.
3. Combine pineapple, wheat germ, onion, butter, soy sauce and rosemary; mix well.
4. Spoon stuffing into cavities; close body cavities.
5. Place hens, breast-side up, on rack in shallow roasting pan. Brush with glaze.
6. Bake uncovered in preheated 350° F. oven 60 to 70 minutes until tender.
7. Brush with glaze about every 15 minutes during baking.

## Honey-Soy Sauce

3 tablespoons honey
2 tablespoons pineapple syrup

1 teaspoon soy sauce
⅛ teaspoon salt

Combine all ingredients; mix well.

# Stuffed Rock Cornish Hen

Serves 2

1½-pound dressed Rock Cornish
   hen, with giblets
salt
pepper
½ teaspoon corn oil
2 tablespoons chopped onion
¾ cup rice, uncooked
½ teaspoon curry powder
1 cup chicken broth

handful seedless raisins
1 tablespoon pine nuts
2 carrots, peeled and cut in
   large cubes
1 small yellow onion, peeled
   and sliced
clusters of red or green grapes
   (for garnish)

1. Rinse hen inside and out; drain well. Season cavity with salt and pepper.
2. Chop giblets. Heat oil in skillet; sauté chopped onions and giblets until onions are limp and giblets are browned, stirring often.
3. Add rice; heat until well coated. Add ⅛ teaspoon salt, curry powder, chicken broth and raisins; cover and simmer 15 to 20 minutes, or until broth is absorbed.
4. Add pine nuts and mix well.
5. Stuff cavity with giblet-rice stuffing. Truss hen and tie legs and wings to body.
6. Place hen in small roasting pan. Arrange carrots and sliced onion around bird. Roast in preheated 350° F. oven 45 minutes, basting several times with pan drippings.
7. Serve garnished with grapes.

# Polynesian Hen

Serves 2

2 tablespoons soy sauce
2 tablespoons orange juice
¼ teaspoon ground ginger
1 teaspoon brown sugar

1 clove garlic, crushed
1 Rock Cornish game hen, weighing
about 1 pound, halved

1. Combine all ingredients except hen in saucepan.
2. Heat mixture gently several minutes.
3. Place hen in glass baking dish; cover with orange juice mixture.
4. Marinate in refrigerator 4 hours, turning occasionally.
5. Remove from marinade; broil about 15 minutes on each side, or roast in preheated 325° F. oven 1 hour.

# Rock Cornish Hen
# with Almond-Prune Stuffing

Serves 1

1 Rock Cornish hen
1 Italian sweet sausage, skinned
3 dried prunes, pitted
¼ cup blanched, slivered almonds
1 thick slice day-old Italian
bread, crustless

½ cup milk
½ teaspoon salt
2 slices lean bacon
freshly ground black pepper
2 tablespoons olive oil
½ cup dry white wine

1. Remove and discard hen's neck; clean and reserve giblets.
2. Cut sausage into small pieces.
3. Cut prunes into quarters.
4. Chop almonds coarsely.
5. Break up and soak bread in milk.
6. Add sausage, giblets and prunes to almonds; chop or process until all ingredients are well chopped and about the same size.
7. Squeeze milk from bread; add bread to stuffing and mix well.
8. Salt hen's cavity, then stuff with almond-prune mixture.
9. Skewer both openings closed.
10. Place bacon on bird's breast; tie wings and legs close to the body. Sprinkle liberally with pepper.
11. Brown hen in oil.
12. Put hen in baking dish. Bake in preheated 400° F. oven 15 minutes.
13. Add wine and baste hen. Lower heat to 375° F. and continue roasting 30 to 40 minutes longer, or until tender.

7

# Rock Cornish Game Hens Baked in Foil

Serves 4

8 strips lean bacon
4 Rock Cornish hens, weighing
about 1 pound each
2 teaspoons salt
½ teaspoon freshly ground black
pepper

1 teaspoon juniper berries, crushed,
or 1 teaspoon gin
1 teaspoon dried tarragon or sage
4 sprigs parsley
3 slices onion, separated into rings
2 cups water

1. Cook bacon over low heat in skillet until it starts to curl; remove to paper towels.
2. Let skillet stand over low heat.
3. Wash and dry hens. Remove bags with giblets and reserve to use for making chicken broth for stock.
4. Mix together salt, pepper, juniper berries and tarragon. Rub hens inside and out with herbed mixture.
5. Cut four 12-inch sheets of aluminum foil. Place a parsley sprig and 3 or 4 onion rings in center of each piece of aluminum foil.
6. Increase heat under skillet; cook hens quickly, browning on all sides.
7. Remove and wrap each hen in foil square.
8. Place wrapped hens in a shallow roasting pan, breast-side down, with water.
9. Moist-roast in preheated 350° F. oven for 1 hour.
10. Remove from oven, open foil carefully, and pour liquid from foil into roasting pan.
11. Increase oven temperature to 425° F.
12. Wrap each bird with 2 slices bacon. Roast, breast-side up, for 10 minutes. Baste with pan juice several times.
13. Remove and keep warm until serving on a heated platter. If desired, strain roasting juices and serve separately in a sauce boat.

NOTE: Stock made from necks, gizzards and livers from hens can be used in lieu of water to moist-roast birds.

# Roast Rock Cornish Hens

Serves 8

4 Rock Cornish hens, weighing
about 1 pound each
1 cup cornflakes, crushed
½ teaspoon tarragon, crushed

½ teaspoon thyme, crushed
¼ teaspoon pepper
1 teaspoon paprika
½ cup milk

½ teaspoon garlic powder

1. Remove skins from game hens. Wash and pat dry.
2. Combine cornflakes, tarragon, thyme, pepper and paprika.
3. Dip hens in milk mixed with garlic powder, then in cornflake mixture.
4. Place on rack in roasting pan. Bake in preheated 375° F. oven 40 to 50 minutes, or until done. Cut in halves.

# Breaded Baked Chicken

Serves 3 to 4

¾ cup fine dry bread crumbs
¼ cup flour
1 teaspoon paprika
1 teaspoon salt
½ teaspoon garlic powder
½ teaspoon freshly grated
   black pepper

½ teaspoon thyme
½ teaspoon oregano
½ teaspoon poultry seasoning
water
1 broiler-fryer chicken, cut
   into serving pieces

1. Combine all ingredients except water and chicken.
2. Moisten chicken with water; roll in crumbs to coat.
3. Put chicken in single layer in baking pan. Bake in preheated 350° F. oven 45 to 60 minutes, or until chicken is fork-tender.

*NOTE: For barbecue-style chicken, dip chicken in barbecue sauce or catsup before rolling in crumbs. Fish and pork may be prepared in this same way too. Fish works better if brushed lightly with melted butter or margarine before coating with crumbs.*

# Chicken Cortez

Serves 6

1 cleaned broiler-fryer chicken,
   weighing 2½ pounds, or 4 chicken
   breasts
¼ cup butter or margarine
2 cups hot water
1 tablespoon instant minced onion
2 teaspoons salt
⅛ teaspoon white pepper
¼ cup cornstarch
2 tablespoons cold water

½ cup ripe olive wedges
½ cup green pepper, diced
1 tablespoon pimiento, chopped
1 tablespoon fresh lemon juice
½ teaspoon crushed rosemary
2 ripe California avocados
4 tablespoons dry sherry
½ square unsweetened chocolate,
   grated

1. Brown chicken in melted butter; add hot water, onion, salt and pepper.
2. Cover and cook over medium heat 35 minutes, or until chicken is tender.
3. Pour off broth and add enough water to make 2 cups.
4. Cut chicken into bite-size pieces.
5. Combine cornstarch and cold water; add to chicken broth. Cook over low heat, stirring constantly until mixture is thickened.
6. Add chicken, ripe olives, green pepper, pimiento, lemon juice and rosemary. Cook over low heat 6 minutes, or until green pepper is just tender.
7. Cut avocados into halves lengthwise; remove seeds and skin. Cut into balls with melon ball cutter or ½ teaspoon measure.
8. Stir avocados into hot chicken mixture with sherry and chocolate. Place over low heat, stirring gently until chocolate melts.

# Baked Dijon Chicken

Serves 4

¼ cup Dijon-style mustard
2 tablespoons shallots, minced
¼ teaspoon tarragon leaves, crushed
⅛ teaspoon Tabasco sauce

5 tablespoons 100% corn oil margarine, melted
1 cleaned broiler-fryer chicken, cut up
¾ cup fine dry bread crumbs

1. Blend together mustard, shallots, tarragon, Tabasco and 1 tablespoon melted margarine in small bowl.
2. Spread mixture over chicken pieces; coat with bread crumbs.
3. Arrange chicken pieces in greased baking dish; drizzle remaining melted margarine over chicken.
4. Bake in preheated 375° F. oven 1 hour, or until done.

# Chicken with 40 Cloves of Garlic

Serves 4 to 6

1 cleaned broiler-fryer chicken, weighing 3 to 4 pounds, cut into serving pieces
4 heads garlic, broken into cloves, but unpeeled
½ cup olive oil
salt to taste
pepper to taste
1 tablespoon mixed herbs: rosemary, thyme, oregano, sage, basil

4 to 6 small boiling potatoes
8 to 10 baby artichokes, trimmed of tough outer leaves
bouquet garni: 1 celery stalk with leaves attached, 2 sprigs parsley, 2 bay leaves, 1 sprig fresh thyme
flour
water
lightly toasted French bread

1. Place chicken, garlic cloves and oil in an earthenware 4 to 6-quart casserole. Season to taste with salt, pepper and herbs.
2. Add potatoes and artichokes; mix well, making certain garlic cloves don't fall to bottom of casserole.
3. Bury bouquet garni in middle.
4. Put ½ cup flour in mixing bowl; add enough cold water to make a stiff paste.
5. Roll out paste on floured board, adding more flour to paste if it seems sticky.
6. Cut paste into long strips, about 1½ inches wide.
7. Moisten lip of casserole; line with dough strips.
8. Moisten inside lip of casserole cover and place on top of casserole. Press dough with fingers to form a firm seal between lid and casserole so no air can escape.
9. Bake in preheated 350° F. oven 1½ hours.
10. Bring unopened casserole to table with a basket of lightly toasted French bread.
11. Break dough seal with a knife. Serve each person some chicken, potato, artichoke hearts and garlic cloves. The garlic, now a soft sweet purée, should be spread on toast or mixed with the vegetables and chicken.

NOTE: Tasty and "slightly" aromatic!

# Broiled Brandied Chicken for Two

¼ cup butter, melted
2 teaspoons brandy flavoring
¼ teaspoon garlic powder

⅛ teaspoon cayenne powder
4 pieces chicken parts
½ teaspoon seasoned salt

hot cooked brown rice (optional)

1. Mix together butter, brandy flavoring, garlic powder and cayenne in shallow dish.
2. Add chicken, turning to coat evenly.
3. Sprinkle with ¼ teaspoon seasoned salt.
4. Place chicken, skin-side up, on small broiler pan. Broil 6 inches from heat about 10 minutes.
5. Turn and brush with remaining butter mixture. Sprinkle with remaining seasoned salt.
6. Broil 15 minutes longer, or until fork can be easily inserted into chicken. Great with hot cooked brown rice.

# Maryland-Style Chicken & Dumplings

Serves 4

1 broiler-fryer chicken,
   weighing 2 to 2½ pounds,
   cut in parts
2 cups water
1 teaspoon salt
¼ teaspoon pepper

6 small onions, peeled
3 sweet potatoes, pared and sliced
3 white potatoes, pared and
   quartered
2 carrots, sliced lengthwise
Dumplings

1. Place chicken, water, salt and pepper in deep saucepan. Cover and simmer 30 minutes.
2. Add vegetables and continue simmering 20 minutes, or until chicken and vegetables are fork-tender.
3. Remove chicken and vegetables from broth; set aside and keep warm.
4. Add enough water to broth to measure 2 quarts; bring to a boil.
5. Drop Dumplings into boiling broth. Cook, uncovered, over medium-high heat, as liquid continues to boil; stir often, until dumplings sink, about 5 minutes.
6. Add Dumplings to chicken and vegetable mixture.

## Dumplings

2 cups all-purpose flour
½ teaspoon salt

2 teaspoons shortening
¾ cup hot water

1. Sift together flour and salt in large bowl.
2. Cut in shortening; stir in hot water until soft dough forms.
3. Roll out dough on a lightly floured surface to 1/16-inch thickness. Cut dough into 1 x 1½-inch rectangles; sprinkle lightly with flour.

# Chicken & Apples Normandy

Serves 4

1 broiler-fryer chicken, weighing
  2½ to 3 pounds, cut into pieces
salt to taste
pepper to taste
3 tablespoons butter or margarine
1 medium onion, thinly sliced
1 clove garlic, minced

½ cup sherry
1 teaspoon chopped parsley
¼ teaspoon dried leaf thyme
2 large Granny Smith apples,
  pared, cored and cut into wedges
½ cup heavy cream
1 cup shredded Swiss cheese

1. Season chicken with salt and pepper.
2. Melt butter in large skillet; add chicken pieces and brown well on all sides.
3. Add onion and garlic; sauté 3 minutes.
4. Add sherry, parsley, ½ teaspoon salt and thyme. Cover and simmer 20 minutes.
5. Add apples and simmer 10 minutes longer, until chicken is tender.
6. Arrange chicken and apples in shallow casserole; set aside.
7. Add cream to skillet; bring to a gentle boil, stirring to dissolve chicken particles.
8. Pour creamed mixture over chicken and apples in casserole; sprinkle with Swiss cheese.
9. Place under preheated broiler until cheese is melted and bubbly. Serve at once.

# Chicken Marengo

Serves 4 to 5

1 broiler-fryer chicken, weighing
  2½ to 3 pounds, cut up
1¼ teaspoon salt
⅛ teaspoon pepper
¼ cup 100% corn oil margarine
2 cups onions, sliced

1 cup mushrooms, sliced
2 cloves garlic, peeled and
  minced
1 can (1 pound) tomatoes
¼ cup dry sherry
2 tablespoons flour

1. Remove excess fat from chicken. Sprinkle chicken with ½ teaspoon salt and pepper.
2. Brown chicken pieces in margarine in a large skillet.
3. Remove from pan; drain on paper towels.
4. Add onions, mushrooms and garlic to skillet. Cook, stirring, until lightly browned.
5. Stir in tomatoes, sherry, remaining salt and chicken. Cover and simmer 30 minutes, until chicken is tender.
6. Drain off and reserve liquid. Chill liquid until fat hardens on surface.
7. Cover and refrigerate chicken mixture.
8. Discard hardened fat from liquid.
9. Blend together flour and small amount of liquid; stir into remaining liquid.
10. Add liquid to chicken mixture. Bring to a boil, stirring.
11. Reduce heat, cover, and cook until chicken is heated through. Serve piping hot.

# Chicken in Mustard Cream

Serves 4

1 whole broiler-fryer, weighing
   3 pounds, skinned and cut into
   serving pieces
¼ pound butter or margarine
1 tablespoon vegetable oil

2 tablespoons fresh or dried rosemary
⅓ cup heavy cream
⅓ cup red wine vinegar
⅓ cup chicken stock
1 tablespoon Dijon mustard

hot cooked rice or pasta (optional)

1. Sauté chicken in butter and oil mixed with rosemary.
2. In separate bowl, whisk together heavy cream, vinegar, chicken stock and mustard.
3. When chicken is one-third cooked, pour sauce over chicken in skillet. Cook, uncovered, turning pieces frequently until chicken is thoroughly cooked. (Juice can be thickened by reduction, if desired.)
4. Serve alone or spooned over hot cooked rice or pasta.

# Coq au Vin, Microwaved

Serves 4 to 6

½ cup flour
2 teaspoons salt
¼ teaspoon freshly ground
   black pepper
1 cleaned broiler-fryer chicken,
   weighing 2½ to 3 pounds,
   cut up
4 slices bacon

2 small onions, peeled and
   thinly sliced
2 stalks celery, diagonally sliced
   into ½-inch pieces
¾ cup red wine
2 tablespoons brandy
1 pound fresh mushrooms, sliced
1 bay leaf

2 tablespoons parsley, chopped

1. Combine flour, salt and pepper in bag. Add chicken pieces; shake to coat. Set aside.
2. Cut bacon in 1-inch pieces. Put bacon in bottom of 3- to 4-quart casserole; microcook, uncovered, on HIGH 3½ minutes.
3. Do not drain bacon; stir in onions and celery. Cook 3 minutes.
4. Add remaining flour from bag, stir until smooth.
5. Gradually add red wine and brandy.
6. Add all remaining ingredients except chicken; stir to mix.
7. Put chicken on top, placing thickest parts toward outside of dish. Cover and microcook 15 to 17 minutes, or until chicken is tender and sauce slightly thickened.
8. Stir gently and microcook, uncovered, 10 to 12 minutes.
9. Remove bay leaf. Cover and let stand 10 minutes before serving.

# Chicken Tarragon, Flambéed

Serves 4

1 cleaned broiler-fryer chicken,
  weighing 2½ to 3 pounds
4 slices lean bacon, diced
4 tablespoons butter
3 shallots, minced

1 cup dry white wine
¼ pound cleaned fresh mushrooms,
  sliced
5 tablespoons tarragon leaves
½ cup brandy

½ cup boiling water

1. Cut up chicken; set aside.
2. Heat bacon slowly with 2 tablespoons butter in a heavy casserole.
3. Increase heat; brown chicken pieces.
4. Stir in shallots until soft.
5. Add wine, mushrooms and 3 tablespoons tarragon leaves. Cover tightly and simmer 25 minutes.
6. Remove lid, raise heat and let liquid evaporate slightly.
7. Warm brandy in a small pan, shaking steadily; ignite brandy, pour over chicken.
8. Stir in boiling water, remaining tarragon leaves and remaining butter.
9. Correct seasoning and serve immediately.

# Cranberry Grilled Chicken

Serves 4

1 can (16 ounces) jellied cranberry
  sauce
½ cup light corn syrup
3 tablespoons cider vinegar
1 tablespoon corn oil

1 teaspoon ground cinnamon
1 teaspoon salt
1 broiler-fryer chicken,
  weighing 2½ to 3 pounds,
  cut in serving pieces

1. Whisk together cranberry sauce, corn syrup, vinegar, corn oil, cinnamon and salt until well blended.
2. Grill chicken 6 inches from source of heat, for 30 minutes, turning frequently.
3. Brush with part of cranberry mixture. Continue grilling, brushing with cranberry mixture and turning frequently, 15 minutes longer, or until chicken is fork-tender.
4. Heat remaining cranberry mixture and serve with chicken.

*NOTE: A pleasant alternative for the small family for holiday dining.*

# Curried Nectarine Chicken

Serves 4

2 tablespoons butter or margarine
2 tablespoons oil
1 broiler-fryer chicken, cut up
2 tablespoons onion, minced
½ teaspoon garlic, minced
⅔ cup nectarines, peeled and chopped
1½ teaspoons curry powder
½ teaspoon cumin
1 chicken bouillon cube, crushed

¾ cup water
1½ tablespoons light brown sugar
1 tablespoon fresh lemon juice
salt to taste
ground black pepper to taste
2 nectarines, sliced
curry accompaniments: shredded
    coconut, salted peanuts, seedless
    green grapes, chutney

1. Heat butter and oil in large skillet. Add chicken and brown slowly on all sides.
2. Remove chicken from skillet.
3. Sauté onion and garlic in skillet drippings.
4. Add chopped nectarines.
5. Mix together curry powder, cumin, bouillon cube, water, brown sugar and lemon juice. Add to skillet and sauté a few minutes.
6. Return chicken to skillet; cover and simmer until chicken is tender, 25 to 35 minutes.
7. Season to taste with salt and pepper.
8. Remove chicken to serving platter and keep warm.
9. Add sliced nectarines to sauce in skillet. Cook over medium heat, just until heated and glazed, about 5 minutes.
10. Pour sauce over chicken and serve with curry accompaniments.

# Dilled Chicken

Serves 4

¼ cup fine-grade olive oil
¼ cup wine vinegar
2 teaspoons sugar (optional)
1 teaspoon dry mustard
1 teaspoon salt
½ teaspoon tarragon leaves
¼ teaspoon rosemary

1 clove garlic, peeled and
    minced
½ teaspoon freshly ground
    black pepper
1 cleaned broiler-fryer chicken
    (about 3 pounds), cut into
    serving pieces

1. Place olive oil, vinegar, sugar, mustard, salt, tarragon, rosemary, garlic and pepper in screw-top pint jar. Cover tightly and shake vigorously.
2. Pour marinade into shallow dish; add chicken, turning several times to coat each piece.
3. Cover and marinate overnight in refrigerator.
4. To cook, place chicken on prepared grill, skin-side up, about 8 inches from heat. Cook, turning every 10 to 15 minutes, for 1 hour, or until fork can be easily inserted in chicken.

# Orange Glazed Chicken

Serves 4 to 6

1 broiler-fryer chicken,
  weighing about 3 pounds,
  cut into serving pieces
1¼ teaspoons salt
¼ cup melted butter or margarine
¼ cup honey

1 can (6 ounces) frozen orange juice
  concentrate, thawed
¾ cup regular wheat germ
¾ cup all-purpose flour
1 teaspoon paprika
¼ teaspoon thyme leaves, crushed

1. Sprinkle chicken pieces with salt; brush with melted butter; set aside.
2. Mix together honey and orange juice concentrate in shallow container.
3. Combine wheat germ, flour, paprika and thyme on waxed paper.
4. Dip chicken pieces into orange juice mixture, then into wheat germ mixture to coat well.
5. Place chicken in single layer on large greased baking pan. Drizzle remaining butter and glaze over chicken.
6. Bake in preheated 375° F. oven 45 to 50 minutes, or until chicken is tender, basting several times during baking.

NOTE: *Three whole chicken breasts, cut in halves, may be used instead of 1 broiler-fryer.*

# Spanish Chicken with Rice

Serves 6

½ cup instant minced onion
¼ cup sweet pepper flakes
⅔ cup water
⅓ cup olive oil
1 broiler-fryer chicken,
  cut into serving pieces
1 can (1 pound 12 ounces)
  tomatoes, broken up
½ cup chopped ham
¼ cup sliced stuffed olives
2½ teaspoons salt

1 teaspoon oregano leaves
½ teaspoon paprika
½ teaspoon freshly ground
  black pepper
½ teaspoon garlic powder
¼ teaspoon saffron
3 cups boiling water
1 cup raw, regular cooking rice
1 package (10 ounces) frozen
  green peas, thawed
pimiento strips (optional garnish)

1. Rehydrate onion and pepper flakes in water for 10 minutes.
2. Meanwhile, heat oil in large saucepan. Add chicken and brown on all sides.
3. Add onion and pepper; sauté 5 minutes.
4. Add tomatoes, ham, olives and seasonings; stir gently.
5. Cover and simmer 10 minutes.
6. Add boiling water and rice; stir.
7. Cover and continue simmering until chicken is almost tender, 20 to 25 minutes.
8. Mix in peas; cook 5 minutes longer.
9. Place in serving casserole. Serve garnished with pimiento strips, if desired.

# Chicken Trinidad

Serves 4

1 broiler-fryer chicken, weighing
   2½ to 3 pounds, quartered
½ cup olive oil
2 cups rice
¼ cup onion, minced
¼ cup green pepper, minced

1 can (4 ounces) mushrooms, undrained
½ teaspoon saffron
2 cups chicken broth (canned or
   homemade)
1 teaspoon Angostura aromatic
bitters

1. Brown chicken in olive oil; remove chicken.
2. Brown rice, onion, and green pepper together.
3. Place rice mixture in bottom of Dutch oven or casserole; top with chicken. Add undrained mushrooms.
4. Dissolve saffron in 1 cup broth; add Angostura and pour into kettle.
5. Cook over low heat, covered, without stirring.
6. After 10 minutes, add second cup broth. Cook additional 15 minutes until rice is dry and fluffy.

# Golden Glazed Chicken

Serves 8

2 broiler-fryer chickens,
   each weighing about 3 pounds,
   cut in quarters
¼ cup butter or margarine
1 tablespoon honey

¼ cup frozen lemonade
   concentrate
1 envelope (1½ ounces)
   sloppy joe seasoning mix

1. Grill or broil chicken over hot coals, or 4 inches from heat, turning frequently until tender.
2. Melt butter; add lemonade, seasoning mix and honey.
3. Brush mixture over chicken; heat until glazed.
4. Serve at once.

# Quartered Chicken Roquefort

Serves 3 to 4

1 broiler-fryer chicken,
   quartered
¼ cup melted butter or margarine
1 tablespoon bottled steak sauce
1 cup dairy sour cream

1 ounce Roquefort cheese,
   crumbled
½ teaspoon salt
pepper to taste
⅛ teaspoon paprika

1. Brush chicken with butter and steak sauce.
2. Place chicken in 2½-quart baking dish.
3. Combine sour cream, cheese, salt, pepper and paprika; pour over chicken.
4. Bake in preheated 325° F. oven about 1½ hours.

*NOTE: Great done with Escoffier sauce too, in lieu of steak sauce!*

17

# Caribbean Chicken

Serves 4

1 broiler-fryer chicken, weighing
2½ to 3 pounds, quartered
¼ cup olive oil
4 medium carrots, scraped and
halved
4 small onions, peeled
3 ripe tomatoes, quartered

½ cup water
2 teaspoons Angostura aromatic
bitters
6 large yams
3 tablespoons butter
½ cup molasses
chopped parsley (for garnish)

1. Brown chicken in olive oil; transfer to Dutch oven.
2. Brown carrots, onions and tomatoes lightly in original oil; add to chicken.
3. Add water and 1 teaspoon Angostura; cover tightly and cook over low heat 20 minutes.
4. Meanwhile, cook yams in boiling water until tender; peel and halve.
5. Melt butter and add molasses and remaining Angostura in separate skillet.
6. Add yams and keep turning in butter-molasses mixture until well glazed and heated through.
7. Spread yams on platter, place chicken and vegetables on top; garnish with parsley.

# "Vinegared" Chicken, French Style

Serves 8

2 cleaned broiler-fryer chickens,
each weighing 2½ to 3 pounds,
quartered
¼ cup butter or margarine
1½ teaspoons salt
½ teaspoon pepper
1 can (10¾ ounces) chicken broth
⅔ cup dry red wine

½ cup tomato purée
⅓ cup red wine vinegar
1 tablespoon minced scallions
1 clove garlic, mashed
1 teaspoon dried tarragon
1 teaspoon sugar
½ bay leaf

1. Brown chicken in butter in 12-inch skillet, removing pieces to roasting pan as they brown.
2. Season chicken in pan with salt and pepper.
3. Drain off most of fat in skillet; add remaining ingredients. Heat to a boil.
4. Pour mixture over chicken in roasting pan. Bake uncovered in preheated 350° F. oven until chicken is tender, about 30 minutes.
5. Remove chicken to heated serving platter; keep warm.
6. Pour pan juices into measuring cup; skim off fat.
7. Pour juices into medium-size saucepan; heat to a boil. Boil until reduced to about 1¼ cups.
8. Pour sauce over chicken.

# Herbed Baked Chicken

Serves 4

1 broiler-fryer chicken,
   quartered
salt to taste
pepper to taste
flour
salad oil

1 teaspoon rosemary, crushed
½ teaspoon basil
½ teaspoon parsley, minced
½ cup orange juice
1½ cups dairy sour cream
4 strips (½ inch wide) orange rind

1. Season chicken with salt and pepper; dredge in flour.
2. Brown chicken on both sides in oil.
3. Arrange chicken in a shallow baking pan. Sprinkle with herbs.
4. Combine orange juice and sour cream; pour over chicken, covering completely.
5. Place one strip of orange rind on each piece of chicken. Cover and bake in preheated 325° F. oven 45 minutes, or until tender.
6. Remove orange rind and bake, uncovered, 5 minutes longer, or until lightly browned.

# Lemoned Chicken

Serves 8

2 broiler-fryer chickens,
   quartered
2 fresh lemons
⅔ cup flour
1 tablespoon salt
1 teaspoon paprika

½ cup corn oil
4 tablespoons brown sugar
2 cups chicken broth or
   bouillon
1 tablespoon Angostura
   aromatic bitters

1. Wash chicken and dry well.
2. Cut 1 lemon in half and squeeze juice from both halves over each chicken piece.
3. Combine flour, salt and paprika in paper bag. Coat chicken by shaking pieces, one at a time, in the bag.
4. Brown chicken parts slowly in oil.
5. Arrange chicken in baking dish or Dutch oven.
6. Thinly slice remaining lemon and place in a layer over chicken.
7. Dissolve brown sugar in chicken broth; add Angostura bitters. Pour over chicken.
8. Cover and bake in preheated 375° F. oven, or simmer over very low flame until chicken is tender, about 1 hour. Serve hot with juice.

# Stuffed Chicken Quarters

Serves 4

½ cup mushrooms, minced
⅓ cup green onion, chopped

prepared barbecue sauce
1½ cups cooked rice

1 broiler-fryer chicken, quartered

1. Combine mushrooms, onion and ¼ cup barbecue sauce in 1-quart saucepan; cook over low heat until vegetables soften.
2. Add rice and heat thoroughly.
3. Loosen skin on each chicken quarter to form a pocket between skin and meat. Spoon vegetable mixture into each pocket; secure with skewers.
4. To cook outdoors, place chicken on greased grill, skin-side up, 5 to 7 inches from coals. Grill over low coals 20 minutes; turn and grill, brushing with barbecue sauce every few minutes.
5. To cook indoors; place chicken, skin-side up, in 12 x 8-inch baking dish; brush with barbecue sauce. Bake in preheated 350° F. oven 1 hour, or until tender, brushing frequently with barbecue sauce.

# Artichoke-Chicken, Oriental Style

Serves 6

2 tablespoons butter or margarine
2 tablespoons salad oil
1 small garlic clove, crushed
2 cups sliced raw chicken pieces (about 2½ pounds broiler-fryer chicken pieces)
3 cups chicken broth or bouillon
¼ cup cornstarch
1 tablespoon soy sauce
2 teaspoons salt

1 cup celery, diagonally sliced
1 can (8½ ounces) bamboo shoots, drained
1 can (9½ ounces) water chestnuts, drained
6 medium artichokes, prepared as directed (see page 24)
blanched, slivered toasted almonds (for garnish)
3 cups hot cooked rice

1. Melt butter in large skillet over medium heat.
2. Add oil, garlic and chicken, stirring constantly until chicken turns white in color.
3. Cover and steam chicken for 5 minutes.
4. Meanwhile, blend chicken broth into cornstarch.
5. Add broth mixture, soy sauce, salt, celery, bamboo shoots and water chestnuts to skillet. Bring mixture to a boil, stirring constantly.
6. Cover and simmer about 10 minutes longer, or until chicken is tender.
7. Fill artichokes, using mainly the chicken and vegetable pieces of mixture, reserving the saucy part of the mixture in a dish as a dip for artichoke leaves.
8. Garnish filled artichokes with almonds and serve with rice.

# Chicken & Rice

Serves 6

2 tablespoons margarine
2 tablespoons vegetable oil
3 pounds chicken parts
1 can (1 pound 3 ounces) tomatoes,
   chopped
1 cup chicken broth
1 cup sliced onion

¼ cup parsley, chopped
2 teaspoons salt
¼ teaspoon pepper
1 bay leaf
1 clove garlic, peeled and minced
1¼ cups uncooked rice
1 package (10 ounces) frozen peas

1. Heat margarine and oil in Dutch oven or large heavy saucepan.
2. Add chicken and brown well.
3. Add tomatoes, chicken broth, onion, parsley, salt, pepper, bay leaf and garlic. Cover and cook over low heat 25 minutes.
4. Add rice and cook 10 minutes, stirring occasionally.
5. Add peas and cook 10 minutes longer, or until done and all liquid is absorbed.

# Chicken, Snow Peas & Cucumber

Serves 4

1 pound boneless skinned chicken,
   cut into ¼-inch cubes
boiling water
1 tablespoon vinegar
1 cucumber
salt

¼ pound snow peas
2 tablespoons soy sauce
3 tablespoons Chinese sesame oil
dash of hot chili oil
½ teaspoon sugar
1 tablespoon sesame seeds, toasted

1. Dip chicken into boiling water; remove after a few seconds.
2. Drain chicken well; sprinkle with vinegar.
3. Halve and seed cucumber; cut into thin slices.
4. Sprinkle cucumber with salt; let stand 30 minutes to draw off water.
5. Rinse and dry cucumber pieces.
6. Slice snow peas on diagonal.
7. Combine remaining ingredients for marinade.
8. Toss chicken and vegetables in marinade; refrigerate until serving time.

*NOTE: Makes a crisp, cold offering for main dish or salad.*

# Country Chicken & Dumplings

Serves 2

4 large pieces chicken
⅔ cup flour
1½ tablespoons corn oil
1 cup chicken broth
2 large carrots, peeled and
    cut in large dices
1 stalk celery with leaves
2 tablespoons chopped onion

1 bay leaf
salt to taste
pepper to taste
1 teaspoon baking powder
3 to 4 tablespoons milk
1½ teaspoons minced
    fresh parsley
⅛ teaspoon ground cloves

1. Dredge chicken in flour. Set flour aside.
2. Heat oil in skillet; brown chicken lightly on all sides.
3. Add broth, carrots, celery, onion, bay leaf, salt and pepper to taste. Cover and simmer 15 minutes.
4. Meanwhile, mix remaining flour with baking powder, ⅛ teaspoon salt, milk, parsley and cloves to make dumpling dough. Spoon into chicken mixture.
5. Cover and simmer 20 minutes, or until dumplings are done.

# Fruited Chicken Dijon

Serves 6

1 can (30 ounces) fruit cocktail
1 green onion, chopped
2 tablespoons parsley, minced
2 teaspoons Dijon-style mustard
grated peel of 1 lemon
juice of ½ lemon
½ teaspoon salt

½ teaspoon pepper
2½ pounds chicken pieces
⅓ cup flour
2 tablespoons corn oil
2 tablespoons butter or margarine
1 chicken bouillon cube
3 cups hot cooked rice

parsley sprigs (optional garnish)

1. Drain fruit cocktail, reserving 1 cup syrup.
2. Mix fruit cocktail, reserved syrup, onion, parsley, mustard, lemon peel and juice, salt and pepper. Set aside.
3. Coat chicken with flour.
4. Heat oil and butter in skillet until hot. Brown chicken over medium heat.
5. Stir in fruit cocktail mixture and bouillon cube. Simmer 20 to 30 minutes, or until chicken is tender.
6. Serve over hot cooked rice. Garnish with parsley sprigs, if desired.

# Orange Chicken

Serves 4

3 pounds chicken parts
½ cup orange juice
¼ cup vegetable oil

1½ teaspoons original Worcester-
    shire sauce
½ teaspoon tarragon leaves, crushed

1. Prick chicken on all sides with fork tines; place in shallow, snug-fitting baking pan.
2. Combine orange juice, oil, Worcestershire sauce and tarragon in a measuring cup; pour over chicken.
3. Cover and marinate chicken 1 hour, turning over after 30 minutes.
4. Bake chicken in preheated 350° F. oven until tender, about 1 hour, basting with orange marinade occasionally.

NOTE: Calories can be reduced more by skinning chicken before marinating.

# Chicken & Rock Lobster, Costa Brava

Serves 8

1 pound frozen South African
    rock lobster tails
salted boiling water
4 whole chicken breasts, split
salt to taste
pepper to taste
¼ cup butter or margarine, melted

2 tablespoons dry sherry
½ pound mushrooms, washed,
    pat-dried and sliced
¼ cup flour
1½ cups chicken broth
2 tablespoons tomato paste
2 tablespoons chives, chopped

3 tomatoes, each cut into 6 wedges

1. Parboil frozen lobster tails by dropping into salted boiling water.
2. When water reboils, drain immediately and drench with cold water.
3. With scissors, remove underside membrane and pull meat out in one piece. Cut each tail into ½-inch-thick crosswise slices.
4. Sprinkle chicken breasts on all sides with salt and pepper; brush with melted butter.
5. Place breasts in large skillet and sprinkle with sherry.
6. Cover skillet tightly and poach chicken in its own juices 30 to 35 minutes, or until breasts are fork-tender.
7. Remove chicken to a heated platter; set aside.
8. Add mushrooms to pan juices and simmer 5 minutes.
9. Mix together flour and chicken broth in a bowl until smooth; stir into mushrooms.
10. Blend in tomato paste and chives; stir over low heat until sauce thickens.
11. Add lobster and tomato wedges to sauce. Simmer 2 minutes until lobster meat is opaque and heated through.
12. Season sauce to taste with salt and pepper. Pour sauce over chicken breasts.
13. Serve hot, with rice pilaf.

# Almond Chicken Casablanca

Serves 8

8 whole chicken breasts,
    split and boned
salad oil
1 cup canned tomato sauce
1 cup water
⅔ cup chopped fresh tomatoes
½ cup slivered almonds, toasted

½ cup dark seedless raisins
1 large clove garlic
2 tablespoons cornstarch
½ tablespoon sugar
scant teaspoon curry powder
½ teaspoon ground cumin
minced fresh parsley

8 cups cooked hot rice

1. Pan-fry chicken breasts in lightly oiled skillet until browned and fork-tender; set aside.
2. Combine tomato sauce, water, tomatoes, almonds, raisins, garlic, cornstarch, sugar, curry powder and cumin in saucepan; stir over medium-high heat until mixture comes to a boil and is thickened. Keep warm.
3. For each serving, spoon about ⅓ cup sauce over 2 chicken breasts. Sprinkle with additional slivered almonds and parsley. Serve with hot cooked rice.

*NOTE: To toast almonds, spread in single layer in shallow pan. Bake in preheated 350° F. oven 10 to 15 minutes, or until almonds begin to turn color. Cool.*

# Artichokes with Sautéed Chicken

Serves 6

4 artichokes
boiling salted water
3 large chicken breasts, boned,
    skinned and halved
salt
¾ cup butter or margarine

1 pound cleaned fresh mushrooms,
    sliced
¼ cup flour
dash white pepper
2 cans (10½ ounces each) condensed
    chicken broth, undiluted

1. Remove 2 or 3 outer layers of artichoke leaves. Cut off stem and top half of each artichoke. Cut in quarters.
2. Cook artichokes in 2 to 3 inches boiling salted water in deep saucepan 15 to 20 minutes, or until tender. Drain and remove chokes (fuzzy portion).
3. Sprinkle chicken lightly on both sides with salt.
4. Melt butter in large skillet; sauté chicken and mushrooms until chicken is browned on both sides. Remove with slotted spoon and set aside.
5. Stir flour and pepper into pan drippings; gradually stir in chicken broth until blended. Boil sauce for 1 minute.
6. Arrange chicken and mushrooms in half of skillet. Add artichokes to other half; baste with sauce.
7. Simmer, covered, 20 minutes, basting occasionally.
8. Serve chicken surrounded with artichokes.

# Avocado-Stuffed Chicken Breasts

Serves 4

1 ripe California avocado,
   peeled and seeded
¼ cup fresh lemon juice
½ cup Monterey Jack cheese,
   shredded

4 chicken breast halves, boned
   and pounded flat
1 egg, beaten
½ cup bread crumbs
1 teaspoon seasoned salt

3 tablespoons butter or margarine

1. Cut avocado in half; cut one half into slices and dip cut edges in lemon juice. Reserve remaining half for garnish.
2. Sprinkle additional lemon juice on skinless side of chicken breasts.
3. Place 2 tablespoons shredded cheese in center of each breast; add avocado slice.
4. Fold breast in half over cheese and avocado slice; press edges to seal.
5. Dip stuffed breasts in egg, then in bread crumbs which have been tossed with seasoned salt.
6. Melt butter in large skillet. Brown chicken on both sides over medium heat.
7. Reduce heat and cook, covered, 15 minutes, or until cooked through.
8. Top with another slice of avocado and serve.

# Chicken & Jicama, Mandarin

Serves 6

1½ pounds boneless chicken
   breasts, cubed
1 tablespoon salad oil
1¾ cups water
2 tablespoons soy sauce
3 chicken bouillon cubes

2 tablespoons cornstarch
2 cups sliced fresh mushrooms
1 cup 1-inch slices peeled jicama
   (available in most supermarkets)
1 cup Chinese pea pods
3 cups hot cooked rice

1. Cook chicken in hot oil in large skillet or wok.
2. Add 1½ cups water, soy sauce and bouillon. Cover and simmer 20 minutes.
3. Mix remaining water with cornstarch; blend into chicken mixture, cooking and stirring until thickened.
4. Add mushrooms, jicama and pea pods. Cook 8 to 10 minutes longer, or just until pea pods are crisp-tender.
5. Serve spooned over hot rice.

NOTE: Jicama is a root vegetable used as an ingredient in salads, stir-fried into Chinese creations, or chopped to add a crisp bite to soups or meat patties. Delightfully low in calories, a 3-ounce portion of jicama provides 45 calories. If unavailable, water chestnuts can be substituted for jicama.

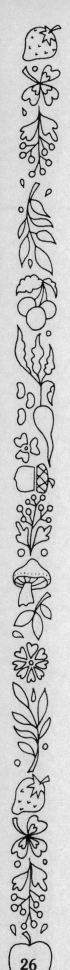

# Chicken Florentine

Serves 2

1 tablespoon corn or olive oil
½ pound boneless chicken,
   chopped
1 can (7 ounces) fruit cocktail,
   drained
1 package (10 ounces) frozen spinach,
   cooked and drained
2 tablespoons butter

2 tablespoons flour
1 cup milk
¼ cup Romano cheese, freshly
   grated
½ teaspoon dried oregano
¼ teaspoon dried basil
¼ teaspoon salt
⅛ teaspoon nutmeg

1. Heat oil in skillet; add chicken. Cook, stirring, until chicken turns white, 3 or 4 minutes.
2. Stir in ¾ cup fruit cocktail.
3. Cook spinach according to package directions; set aside.
4. Heat butter in small saucepan; stir in flour, cooking until smooth.
5. Gradually stir in milk; cook, stirring constantly, until thickened.
6. Stir in remaining ingredients.
7. Mix ¼ sauce into spinach and spread on bottom of shallow 1-quart casserole.
8. Arrange chicken-fruit cocktail mixture over spinach. Pour remaining sauce over chicken mixture.
9. Sprinkle with additional cheese, if desired.
10. Bake in preheated 400° F. oven 20 minutes, or until hot.

# Chicken Kiev

Serves 4

4 whole chicken breasts
salt
pepper
1 cube sweet butter, softened

1 teaspoon fresh parsley, minced
garlic powder (optional)
2 eggs, beaten
bread crumbs

vegetable oil for frying

1. Remove bones from chicken. Cut breasts in half; pound flat and thin. Sprinkle each piece with salt and pepper.
2. Blend softened butter with parsley and garlic powder to taste.
3. Roll mixture into egg shape; chill before using.
4. Cut butter mixture into 8 equal parts (one for each cutlet).
5. Place butter mixture in center of each piece of chicken. Roll up and fold flaps in. Fasten each end with half a wood toothpick.
6. Roll cutlets into beaten eggs, then in bread crumbs. Coat heavily and let stand at least 15 minutes before frying, or refrigerate until ready, even hours, if need be.
7. Brown cutlets in 1 inch of oil at moderate heat carefully, without crowding them in pan.
8. Remove gently and drain on paper towels.
9. Bake in preheated 350° F. oven 8 to 10 minutes.

# Danish Chicken Breasts

Serves 10

5 boneless chicken breasts, skinned
10 pieces cream cheese with herbs and spices, cut into ½ x 3-inch strips

2 eggs, lightly beaten
¼ teaspoon salt
2 cups fine soft bread crumbs
¼ cup vegetable oil
2 tablespoons butter or margarine

1. On underside of each breast, tuck a strip of cream cheese beneath the long, thin muscle, or make a pocket with a sharp knife.
2. Blend eggs and salt in mixing bowl. Dip chicken into egg, then coat with bread crumbs.
3. Heat oil and butter in skillet or electric frying pan. Brown chicken quickly on skin side about 1 minute, then turn to crown on reverse side.
4. Transfer to baking pan, cheese-side down. Bake in preheated 350° F. oven 20 minutes.

*VARIATION: Use turkey breast slices.*

# Country-Skillet Chicken

Serves 4

5 large cloves fresh garlic
1 tablespoon fresh lemon juice
4 large pieces frying chicken: breasts or thighs plus drumstick portions
2 tablespoons butter
1 tablespoon vegetable oil
1 cup halved or sliced fresh mushrooms

½ cup Chablis or other dry white wine
1 bay leaf
½ teaspoon salt
1 teaspoon Dijon mustard
½ cup chicken broth
1 tablespoon chopped fresh parsley

1. Peel garlic. Finely mash 1 clove garlic or put through garlic press.
2. Mix with lemon juice and rub over chicken pieces. Let stand 10 minutes.
3. Melt butter with oil over medium low heat. Add chicken pieces; sauté 15 minutes, turning once.
4. Add mushrooms, wine, bay leaf, salt and remaining 4 whole cloves garlic. Cover and cook 10 minutes.
5. Blend mustard with chicken broth. Pour over chicken and continue cooking, covered, until chicken is tender, 10 to 15 minutes longer.
6. Remove chicken and whole garlic cloves to serving platter and keep warm.
7. Discard bay leaf. Bring pan liquid to a boil and cook rapidly a few minutes to reduce and thicken slightly.
8. Pour over chicken; sprinkle with parsley.
9. Serve a whole clove of soft-cooked garlic with each portion, to mash into sauce as chicken is eaten.

*NOTE: This is a fabulous example of French country cooking from Provence.*

# Haitian Coconut Chicken

Serves 4

8 chicken breast halves,
   skinned and boned
2 cups all-purpose flour
1 tablespoon salt
2 teaspoons black pepper
3 to 4 tablespoons paprika
⅓ cup peanut oil
2 onions, peeled and sliced
1 large green pepper,
   cut in strips

1 can (16 ounces) tomatoes
¾ teaspoon curry powder
pinch saffron
½ cup shredded unsweetened
   coconut
3 cups chicken stock
2 cups hot cooked rice
chutney

1. Dredge chicken in flour mixed with salt, pepper and 2 teaspoons paprika.
2. Brown in oil on both sides in heavy skillet.
3. Remove chicken to heated platter.
4. Sauté onions, pepper, tomatoes, curry, saffron and remaining paprika in pan drippings.
5. Add chicken to skillet; cook 10 to 15 minutes, or until chicken is tender.
6. While chicken is cooking, mix together coconut and chicken stock; simmer 10 minutes.
7. Add stock mixture to chicken. Cook to reduce liquid slightly to make its own gravy.
8. Serve chicken over rice. Spoon sauce over chicken. Serve chutney on the side.

# Marinated Chicken with Rosemary

Serves 4

4 chicken breasts, steamed 10 to
   15 minutes, until cooked through
juice of ½ large lemon
¼ cup fine-grade olive oil
1 teaspoon rosemary, crushed

salt to taste
pepper to taste
1 tomato, diced
1 scallion, diced
soy sauce (optional)

1. Skin, bone, and dice chicken breasts as soon as cool enough to handle.
2. Toss diced chicken with lemon juice, olive oil, rosemary, salt and pepper. Refrigerate until cold.
3. Just before serving, toss with tomato and scallion.
4. Adjust seasonings if necessary. If desired, toss with small amount of soy sauce to flavor chicken more.

NOTE: Delicious for hot weather dining.

# Marinated Chicken Veronique

Serves 4

4 half chicken breasts, skinned
  and boned
Marinade
¾ pound fresh California grapes
  (blue-black, red or green), stemmed

2 tablespoons butter
2 tablespoons corn oil
1¼ cups heavy cream
parsley sprigs (for garnish)
hot cooked rice

1. Cut each chicken breast diagonally into 4 or 5 strips. Put in bowl with Marinade. Let stand 5 minutes.
2. Meanwhile, halve grapes and seed, if necessary. Set aside.
3. Heat butter and oil in skillet. Remove chicken pieces from marinade (reserving marinade) and sauté quickly, 2 minutes per side.
4. Remove chicken from pan and keep warm.
5. Deglaze pan with ¼ cup water. Stir cream into remaining marinade in bowl; then pour mixture into pan.
6. Cook and stir mixture over medium heat to thicken slightly.
7. Put chicken and grapes into sauce. Heat through. Taste for seasonings.
8. Pour into heated bowl. Garnish with parsley sprigs. Serve with hot rice.

## Marinade

2 tablespoons cornstarch
3 tablespoons sherry

1 tablespoon soy sauce
½ teaspoon ginger
1 clove garlic, mashed

Combine cornstarch, sherry, soy sauce, ginger and garlic. Mix.

# Roma Chicken

Serves 6

3 large boneless chicken
  breasts, skinned and pounded
salt
pepper
3 tablespoons butter

1 tablespoon flour
½ cup milk
2 tablespoons freshly grated
  Parmesan cheese
2 tablespoons grated Swiss cheese

snipped parsley

1. Rub chicken cutlets with salt and pepper.
2. Brown on both sides in 2 tablespoons butter; set aside.
3. Melt remaining butter. Stir in flour and add milk.
4. Bring to a boil. Keep stirring until thick and smooth, about 10 minutes.
5. Add Parmesan and Swiss cheeses to mixture.
6. Place chicken in buttered shallow baking pan; spread each piece with cheese sauce.
7. Brown in preheated 450° F. oven about 10 minutes. Serve piping hot, topped with snipped parsley.

NOTE: Boneless breast of turkey works equally well in lieu of chicken.

29

# Chicken Pistachio Italiano

Serves 8

8 boneless chicken breasts
salt
freshly ground black pepper
flour
1 egg, beaten
⅓ cup milk

1½ cups pistachio nuts, chopped
⅓ cup fresh bread crumbs
½ cup plus 2 tablespoons Parmesan
    cheese, freshly grated
6 tablespoons butter or margarine
1 cup heavy cream

1. Lightly pound breasts to flatten. Season both sides generously with salt and pepper.
2. Dip in flour; shake off excess.
3. Combine egg and milk; dip breasts into mixture.
4. Combine nuts, bread crumbs and ½ cup Parmesan cheese.
5. Dip breasts in nut-cheese mixture.
6. Melt ¼ cup butter in heavy skillet. Sauté chicken on both sides until golden, 3 to 4 minutes per side.
7. Remove breasts to heated platter.
8. Add heavy cream to skillet; cook over low heat to reduce to thick syrupy consistency.
9. Add remaining butter and cook, stirring, until smooth.
10. Blend in remaining cheese. Serve sauce over chicken.

# Chicken Supreme

Serves 6 to 8

3 pounds chicken breasts
1 cup melted butter
1 medium onion, peeled and sliced
salt to taste
pepper to taste
½ pound fresh mushrooms
½ cup flour
3 cups chicken broth

1½ cups light cream
½ cup dry sherry
2 tablespoons fresh lemon juice
½ teaspoon nutmeg
1 package (3 pounds) frozen artichoke
    hearts, thawed (for garnish)
1 cup toasted slivered
    almonds (for garnish)

pitted ripe olives (for garnish)

1. Bone and split chicken breasts.
2. Melt ½ cup butter in skillet; sauté onions until transparent. Remove onions from butter.
3. Sauté chicken breasts until light and golden brown. Salt and pepper to taste.
4. Sauté mushrooms and set aside.
5. Melt remaining butter; gradually add flour, chicken broth and cream. Cook until thick and smooth, stirring constantly.
6. Add sherry, lemon juice and nutmeg.
7. Add chicken and mushrooms.
8. To serve, garnish with artichoke hearts, toasted almonds and olives.

# Chicken Livers Normandie

Serves 2

1 green apple, cored and cut in
  eight wedges
2 tablespoons butter or margarine
½ pound whole chicken livers,
  cut in half
seasoned flour

1 tablespoon dry red wine
2 scallions with tops, sliced
1 cup cooked rice, cooked in chicken
  broth
2 to 3 tablespoons seedless raisins
1 tablespoon toasted sliced almonds

dash black pepper

1. Cook apple wedges in 1 tablespoon butter until soft. Remove from pan; keep warm.
2. Lightly dredge chicken livers in seasoned flour.
3. Melt remaining butter in pan in which apples were cooked; sauté livers about 10 minutes.
4. Add wine, apples and scallions; cover and cook 5 minutes longer to blend flavors.
5. Combine remaining ingredients in a saucepan and heat thoroughly.
6. Toss lightly and serve livers and apples on mounds of hot rice.

# Sautéed Chicken Livers

Serves 2

½ cup chopped onion
¼ pound cleaned fresh mushrooms,
  sliced
3 to 4 tablespoons vegetable oil
  or butter

½ pound chicken livers, with
  lobes separated
¼ teaspoon dried tarragon,
  crushed
salt to taste

pepper to taste

1. Sauté onion and mushrooms in vegetable oil over low heat for 5 minutes, or until onion has softened.
2. Add chicken livers; increase heat to medium. Sauté chicken livers until outsides are browned and insides are still pink, about 5 minutes.
3. Season with tarragon, and salt and pepper to taste. Toss gently to mix with seasonings.
4. Great served with sliced beefsteak tomatoes and butter-toasted split English muffins.

31

# Walnut Chicken with Lime Sauce

Serves 6

6 large chicken half breasts,
   boned and skinned
salt to taste
pepper to taste

2 egg whites
1 cup California walnuts,
   finely chopped
Lime Sauce

1. Season chicken with salt and pepper.
2. Beat egg whites lightly.
3. Dip chicken in egg white, turning to coat. Drain well, then roll in walnuts.
4. Place chicken in buttered baking pan. Bake in preheated 350° F. oven 20 to 25 minutes, until chicken is cooked through.
5. Serve hot, with Lime Sauce.

NOTE: Elegantly simple!

## Lime Sauce

Makes about 1⅓ cups

2 tablespoons butter
2 tablespoons flour
1 cup chicken broth
½ teaspoon salt

dash white pepper
2 egg yolks
2 eggs
½ teaspoon lime peel, grated

2 tablespoons fresh lime juice

1. Melt butter; stir in flour.
2. Add chicken broth, salt and white pepper. Cook, stirring, until mixture boils thoroughly.
3. Beat egg yolks with whole eggs. Stir hot sauce into eggs.
4. Return mixture to very low heat and stir constantly until thickened.
5. Remove from heat; blend in lime peel and lime juice.

# Soyed Chicken Wings

Serves 6 to 8

2 packages (1 pound each) chicken
   wings
1½ teaspoons ground ginger
¼ cup dry white wine

¼ cup sugar
¼ cup soy sauce
½ cup water
1 chicken bouillon cube

1. Place chicken wings in stockpot. Sprinkle with ginger and wine.
2. Cover and simmer over medium-high heat until wine is almost evaporated.
3. Add remaining ingredients, mixing well.
4. Simmer and cook, covered, 1 hour, stirring wings often and keeping heat medium to medium-high.

NOTE: Delicious to serve as first or main course. Inexpensive too!

# Chicken Supreme Crêpes, Microwaved

Serves 6

¼ cup corn oil margarine
1½ cups mushrooms, sliced
⅓ cup flour
1 cup chicken broth
1 cup milk

2 tablespoons Parmesan cheese, grated
¼ teaspoon onion powder
2 cups cooked chicken, diced
⅓ cup sliced pitted ripe olives
12 prepared Basic Crêpes

1. Melt margarine in a 1-quart casserole for 30 seconds on HIGH.
2. Add mushrooms; cook 1 minute.
3. Remove mushrooms from dish; set aside.
4. Alternately mix flour and part of chicken broth into liquid left in casserole, making a smooth paste.
5. Stir in remaining broth, milk, cheese and onion powder. Cook 6 minutes, stirring every 2 minutes.
6. Set 1 cup sauce aside.
7. Mix mushrooms, chicken and olives into remaining sauce.
8. Spread Basic Crêpes flat; spoon ¼ cup chicken mixture into each one.
9. Arrange crêpes on six small serving dishes. Heat half for 3 minutes; repeat with remaining crêpes.
10. Heat reserved sauce 1 minute. Pour sauce equally over crêpes before serving.

## Basic Crêpes

Makes 14 to 16 crêpes

⅔ cup milk
⅔ cup water
2 eggs
1 egg yolk

1½ cups sifted all-purpose flour
¼ teaspoon salt
2 tablespoons melted butter or margarine

1. Combine milk, water, eggs and egg yolk in blender container.
2. Add flour, salt, and melted butter; blend at low speed.
3. Heat 8-inch crêpe pan over high heat.
4. Remove pan from heat; brush lightly with melted butter.
5. Pour in a scant 3 tablespoons batter, tilting pan to thinly coat bottom.
6. Return to heat. When crêpe is lightly browned, turn and brown other side.

# Chicken Lasagna

Serves 10 to 12

6 chicken breasts, cooked
2 cans (10 ounces each) tomatoes
  with jalapeno chilies
1 can (2¼ ounces) sliced olives
8 eight-inch flour tortillas

2 large California avocados,
  peeled and sliced
2 cups dairy sour cream
1½ pounds Monterey Jack
  cheese, shredded

1. Remove skin and bones from chicken. Shred meat with fingers.
2. Combine tomatoes and olives, lightly crushing tomatoes with back of spoon.
3. Spread thin layer of tomato mixture in bottom of a 13 x 9-inch baking pan.
4. Arrange 4 tortillas over tomatoes, overlapping as needed to cover bottom of pan.
5. Add another layer of half the tomato-olive mixture.
6. Add a layer of half the chicken, then half the avocado slices, using a rubber spatula or the back of a spoon.
7. Add layer of half the sour cream; sprinkle with half the cheese.
8. Repeat layers.
9. Bake, uncovered, in preheated 375° F. oven 35 to 45 minutes. Cut into squares to serve.

# Chicken Tacos

Makes 10 tacos

3 tablespoons 100% corn oil margarine
2 whole cooked chicken breasts, boned,
  skinned and cut into thin strips
1 cup onion, chopped
1 clove garlic, peeled and minced
1 can (1 pound) whole tomatoes, chopped
½ teaspoon chili powder
½ teaspoon salt

¼ teaspoon pepper
¼ teaspoon Tabasco sauce
1 tablespoon cornstarch dissolved in
  2 tablespoons water
½ cup sliced ripe olives
¼ cup parsley, chopped
10 taco shells, heated
shredded lettuce

1. Melt margarine in large skillet over medium heat; brown chicken.
2. Add onion and garlic; cook until tender.
3. Stir in tomatoes, chili powder, salt, pepper and Tabasco. Simmer 2 to 3 minutes.
4. Add dissolved cornstarch; heat until mixture thickens, stirring frequently.
5. Stir in olives and parsley. Heat 2 to 3 minutes.
6. To serve, fill taco shell with about ½ cup chicken mixture. Top with shredded lettuce.

# Honey Soyed Roast Chicken with Apple-Bulgur Stuffing

Serves 6

## For Stuffing

1 large yellow onion, peeled and minced
¼ cup butter
1 cup bulgur (cracked wheat)
2 cups peeled, minced tart apples
½ cup minced prunes

¼ teaspoon thyme
¼ teaspoon sage
¼ teaspoon celery seed
salt to taste
pepper to taste
2 cups apple cider
1 tablespoon minced parsley

1. Sauté onion in heavy pot in butter until limp.
2. Add bulgur and apples; stir-fry 2 to 3 minutes, or until golden.
3. Add remaining ingredients and bring to a boil for 3 minutes.
4. Turn off heat, cover pan, and let sit undisturbed 20 to 25 minutes.
5. Fluff mixture with fork.

## To Stuff and Cook Bird

1 cleaned roasting chicken or capon, weighing 4 to 5 pounds
¼ cup honey
¼ cup dark soy sauce
kumquats (for garnish)

salt (optional)
pepper (optional)
pickled crab apples (for garnish)
cooked prunes (for garnish)

1. Wipe bird with damp cloth.
2. Fill cavity ¾ with Apple-Bulgur Stuffing, filling upper cavity as well as body of bird.
3. Close openings with skewers or by stitching.
4. Tie ends of drumsticks together so they will be close to body; turn wings back, passing a string around bird to keep them flat.
5. Place bird on greased rack in roasting pan, breast-side up. Roast in preheated 325° F. oven, allowing 20 minutes per pound, or until internal temperature registers 185° F. on meat thermometer.
6. Meanwhile, prepare glaze by mixing together honey and soy sauce.
7. Brush bird every 10 minutes during last hour of roasting time. (If deep brown glaze is desired, increase oven temperature to 450° F. during last 15 minutes of roasting time.)
8. When bird is done, remove skewers and string. Garnish serving platter with pickled crab apples, cooked prunes and kumquats.

NOTE: Sensational tasting and looking!

# Plain Roasted Chicken

Serves 4

1 whole cleaned broiler-fryer chicken, weighing 2½ to 3 pounds
1 teaspoon salt

¼ teaspoon freshly ground black pepper
plums, pickled peaches, crab apples, watercress or parsley (optional garnishes)

1. Wash and dry chicken carefully.
2. Mix together salt and pepper; sprinkle over outside and inside of chicken.
3. If desired, fill chicken cavity with your favorite stuffing.
4. Hook wing tips onto back.
5. Place chicken, breast-side up, on rack in shallow baking pan. Roast in preheated 375° F. oven 1 hour, or until fork can be inserted in chicken with ease and leg moves freely when lifted or twisted.
6. If bird is stuffed, add 15 minutes to total cooking time.
7. Remove to heated platter. Allow 10 minutes before carving.
8. Garnish with plums, pickled peaches, crab apples, watercress or parsley, if desired.

# Plum-Wonderful Roasted Chicken

Serves 4

1¼ cups herb bread stuffing
1 apple, minced
⅓ cup celery, minced
9 tablespoons hot water
3 tablespoons margarine, melted
2 tablespoons walnuts, chopped
1 tablespoon onion, grated

1 cleaned broiler-fryer chicken, weighing 2½ to 3 pounds
½ cup dry white wine
½ cup plum jam
¼ cup fresh lemon juice
1½ teaspoons ground ginger
½ teaspoon salt

2 tablespoons flour

1. Mix together stuffing, apple, celery, 5 tablespoons water, margarine, walnuts, and onion in large mixing bowl.
2. Spoon into cavity of chicken.
3. Hook wing tips onto back; tie legs together.
4. Place chicken in large shallow baking pan.
5. Make plum sauce by mixing together wine, jam, lemon juice, ginger and salt in mixing bowl.
6. Pour sauce over chicken, brushing to coat.
7. Bake, uncovered, in preheated 350° F. oven, basting occasionally, 1¾ hours, or until leg moves freely when lifted or twisted.
8. Remove chicken to heated serving platter.
9. Skim and discard fat from juices in pan.
10. Mix flour and remaining water in small mixing bowl; blend until smooth.
11. Add flour mixture to juices in baking pan; cook, stirring, over medium heat 5 minutes, or until thick. Serve with chicken.

# Old-Fashioned Chicken Pudding

Serves 6

1 roasting chicken, weighing about
  6 pounds, cut up
4 cups water
1 onion, sliced
2 cups celery and leaves, sliced
¼ cup parsley, chopped
1 teaspoon salt

1 tablespoon Angostura aromatic bitters
1 teaspoon poultry seasoning
4 eggs
1½ cups milk
1¾ cups sifted all-purpose flour
1½ teaspoons salt
¼ cup butter or margarine, melted

1. Combine chicken, water, onion, celery and leaves, parsley, salt, Angostura and poultry seasoning in a large saucepan.
2. Cover and simmer until chicken is tender, about 1 to 1½ hours.
3. Remove chicken and vegetables to 2½-quart casserole. Reserve broth.
4. Beat eggs with milk, flour, salt and melted butter in a bowl until smooth. Pour batter evenly over chicken pieces.
5. Bake in preheated 450° F. oven 15 minutes.
6. Lower heat to 350° F.; bake 20 to 25 minutes longer, or until pudding is puffed and brown.
7. Boil reserved broth to reduce to 3 cups.
8. Mix an additional 6 tablespoons butter and an additional 6 tablespoons flour in a bowl until a smooth paste is formed.
9. Drop lump of paste into broth; stir over low heat until sauce thickens.
10. Season to taste with additional salt and pepper.
11. Spoon pudding onto serving plates; spoon hot gravy over each serving.

# Roast Tarragon Chicken à la Française

Serves 4 to 6

5-pound ready-to-cook roasting
  chicken
2 tablespoons fresh lemon juice
2½ teaspoons salt

½ cup butter or margarine,
  softened
1½ teaspoons tarragon leaves,
  crumbled

1. Brush chicken inside and out with lemon juice mixed with salt.
2. Mix butter with tarragon; generously rub into skin of chicken, as well as inside cavity.
3. Place chicken, breast-side up, on rack in roasting pan. Roast in preheated 375° F. oven 1 hour and 20 minutes, or until done; baste occasionally with pan drippings.
4. Serve with pan-roasted potatoes. Equally good served cold with a salad.

# Harvest-Time Capon
# with Old-Fashioned Bread Stuffing

Serves 6 to 8

## For the Capon

1 frozen capon, weighing
  5 to 8 pounds, thawed
½ teaspoon salt
melted butter, margarine or oil

Old-Fashioned Bread Stuffing
sliced tomatoes (optional garnish)
sliced cucumbers (optional garnish)
greens (optional garnish)

1. Remove plastic bag from capon; free legs and tail from tucked position. Remove giblets from body and neck cavities.
2. Rinse capon inside and outside under cold running water; pat-dry with paper toweling. Sprinkle cavities with salt.
3. Fill cavities loosely with stuffing, allowing 1 cup stuffing for each pound of capon.
4. Skewer neck skin to back. Return legs and tail to tucked position or cover stuffing with aluminum foil and tie legs and tail together loosely.
5. Place capon, breast-side up, on rack in shallow open roasting pan. (Use no water in pan.) Cover capon loosely with aluminum foil, crimping it to edges of pan; roast in preheated 325° F. oven, allowing 40 minutes per pound.
6. Remove foil 30 to 45 minutes before end of roasting time; brush skin with butter. Cut band of skin or string to free legs.
7. Roast until leg joint moves easily and meat is tender.
8. Arrange on platter; garnish with tomato and cucumber slices and greens.

## Old-Fashioned Bread Stuffing

Makes about 6 cups

¾ cup butter or margarine
2½ cups celery, diced
1 cup onion, chopped
1½ to 2 teaspoons poultry seasoning

1 teaspoon salt
10 cups day-old or toasted bread cubes
1 egg, beaten slightly
¼ cup hot water

1. Melt butter in large skillet.
2. Add celery and onion; sauté 3 to 4 minutes and stir in seasonings.
3. Combine all ingredients in a large bowl; mix gently.
4. Stuff capon as directed.

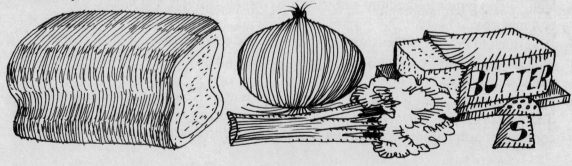

# Broccoli Capon Casserole with Cream Sauce

Serves 8 to 10

## Casserole

cooked meat from a 7- to 8-pound capon, deboned and cut into bite-size chunks
3 boxes frozen broccoli, partly cooked

cream sauce
1 cup sharp cheese, shredded
1½ cups stuffing cubes, seasoned
4 tablespoons melted butter

1. Layer capon pieces and broccoli in casserole; pour Cream Sauce mixture over all.
2. Sprinkle with cheese, stuffing cubes, and melted butter; cover casserole with aluminum foil and bake in preheated 350° F. oven 1 hour, removing foil after ½ hour.

## Cream Sauce

3 cans (10¾ ounces each) condensed cream of mushroom soup
½ cup milk
1 cup real mayonnaise

1 teaspoon fresh lemon juice
½ teaspoon curry powder
⅔ to 1 cup capon broth (made from giblets and neck), or chicken broth

Mix together mushroom soup, milk, mayonnaise, lemon juice, curry powder and capon broth; skim off fat.

# Roast Capon with Mushroom-Almond Stuffing

Serves 4 to 6

1 cleaned capon, weighing 5 to 6 pounds
salt
pepper
3 cups dry white bread cubes
3 cups dry whole wheat bread cubes
1 cup slivered almonds

¼ cup parsley, chopped
1 teaspoon tarragon
butter
2 cups fresh mushrooms, sliced
½ cup onion, chopped
½ cup chicken stock

1. Rinse capon with cold water, drain and pat-dry. Lightly season with salt and pepper.
2. Stir together bread cubes, almonds, parsley, tarragon, 1½ teaspoons salt and ½ teaspoon pepper.
3. Melt ¼ cup butter in medium-size skillet. Cook mushrooms and onions until tender, 3 or 4 minutes.
4. Add stock to mushroom mixture; pour over bread cubes and stir until moistened.
5. Stuff front and inside cavity of bird with dressing. Fasten opening with picks or poultry pins; tie drumsticks together.
6. Place capon on rack in roasting pan; dot with butter. Roast, uncovered, in preheated 325° F. oven, allowing 40 minutes per pound. Brush often with melted butter and continue roasting until leg joint moves easily. Serve on warm platter.

# Roast Capon with Almond Stuffing

Serves 6 to 8

1 frozen capon, weighing 6 to
8 pounds, defrosted
2 teaspoons salt
½ cup butter or margarine
1½ cups celery, thinly sliced
½ cup onion, minced
¾ cup hot water

5 cups cubed crust-free bread, toasted
½ teaspoon poultry seasoning
(optional)
½ cup toasted, slivered almonds
2 eggs, lightly beaten
fruits to garnish platter: green grapes,
oranges, peaches, papaya or avocados

1. Wash, drain, and pat capon dry with paper toweling. Sprinkle inside cavities of capon with 1½ teaspoons salt.
2. To prepare stuffing, melt butter in skillet. Add celery, onion, water and remaining salt.
3. Cover and cook over moderate heat until vegetables are almost tender, stirring frequently, about 5 minutes.
4. Combine bread cubes, poultry seasoning and nuts; mix.
5. Stir in vegetables and liquid; mix.
6. Stir in eggs.
7. Stuff neck and body cavities loosely with bread mixture. Skewer neck skin to back. Return legs and tail to tucked position or tie legs together loosely.
8. Place capon, breast-side up, on rack in shallow roasting pan. Brush skin with melted butter.
9. Cover loosely with aluminum foil, crimping it to edges of pan. Place in preheated 325° F. oven and roast 3½ to 4 hours.
10. Remove foil 45 minutes before end of roasting time. Brush capon with melted butter and continue roasting until leg joints move easily.
11. To serve, place capon on platter and garnish with an attractive assortment of favorite fruits and nuts.

# Capon with Sesame-Barley Stuffing

Serves 4 to 6

1 frozen capon, weighing 6 to 8 pounds
1 jar (1⅛ ounces) sesame seeds
½ cup celery, minced
¼ cup onion, minced
¼ cup butter or margarine
1 tablespoon parsley flakes

1½ teaspoons salt
1 teaspoon poultry seasoning
¼ teaspoon pepper
4 cups cooked barley (2 cups
uncooked barley)

1. Thaw capon according to directions on wrapper.
2. Place sesame seeds in shallow skillet; toast in preheated 350° F. oven 15 to 20 minutes, stirring occasionally for uniform toasting.
3. Cook celery and onion in butter in skillet until tender.
4. Combine with remaining ingredients; mix well.
5. Stuff bird and roast according to directions on wrapper.

# Glazed Capon with Kasha Stuffing & Orange Glaze

Serves 6 to 8

1 cleaned capon, weighing
   4 to 5 pounds
1½ cups kasha (buckwheat
   groats), uncooked
4 eggs
3 cups orange juice
1½ teaspoons salt
¼ teaspoon pepper

3 tablespoons margarine
1½ cups onion, chopped
1½ cups mushrooms, chopped
1 clove garlic, minced
⅓ cup seedless raisins
1 teaspoon seasoned salt
Orange Glaze
2 teaspoons flour

¾ cup water

1. Wash capon inside and out; pat dry.
2. Mix kasha with 2 lightly beaten eggs in mixing bowl.
3. Cook kasha in a large skillet over high heat, stirring constantly, until kasha is dry and each grain is separated.
4. Bring orange juice to a boil in saucepan. Add salt and pepper; mix well.
5. Pour juice over kasha in skillet; cover and simmer 15 to 20 minutes, or until orange juice is absorbed and kasha is tender.
6. Melt margarine in a medium-size skillet; sauté onion, mushrooms and garlic until golden.
7. Add raisins and remaining lightly beaten eggs.
8. Stir onion-raisin mixture into cooked kasha.
9. Spoon kasha stuffing loosely into cavity and neck of capon, filling a small casserole dish with the remaining stuffing.
10. Sprinkle capon with seasoned salt and place on a rack, breast-side up, in shallow roasting pan. Roast in preheated 350° F. oven 30 minutes.
11. Brush with Orange Glaze and continue roasting 1 hour longer, or until capon is done, brushing often with glaze during roasting.
12. Bake stuffing, uncovered, during the last 45 minutes of capon roasting.
13. Remove capon from roasting pan and place on serving platter.
14. Skim fat from pan drippings. Place roasting pan over low heat; stir flour into pan drippings.
15. Gradually add water; stir constantly until gravy boils and thickens. Season to taste.

## Orange Glaze

Makes ⅔ cup

⅓ cup frozen orange juice concentrate,
   thawed and undiluted
⅓ cup water

1 teaspoon seasoned salt
1 clove garlic, peeled
   and minced

1. Combine orange juice concentrate, water, seasoned salt and garlic; mix well.
2. Use to brush on capon.

# Smokey Nectarine Glaze for Duckling or Chicken

Makes about 2 cups

6 to 8 fresh California nectarines
¼ cup sugar
¼ cup corn syrup
¼ cup catsup
2 tablespoons vinegar

1 tablespoon onion, grated
1 teaspoon salt
½ teaspoon liquid smoke (optional)
¼ teaspoon allspice
butter

1. Peel and slice nectarines; mash or whirl in blender to make 2 cups purée.
2. Pour into large saucepan; add remaining ingredients except butter. Simmer 5 to 10 minutes.
3. Use to glaze duckling, chicken or ham, brushing several times over meat while roasting shortly before removing from heat.
4. Stir 1 or 2 tablespoons butter into remaining glaze and serve hot as sauce.

# Duckling with Mole Sauce

Serves 6 to 8

2 cleaned ducklings, weighing 4 to 5
  pounds each, quartered
1 teaspoon salt
1 cup onion, chopped
1 clove garlic, peeled and minced
2 tablespoons corn oil
½ cup tomato sauce
¼ cup raisins

¼ cup creamy-style peanut butter
2 teaspoons sugar
1 teaspoon chili powder
¼ teaspoon cinnamon
dash ground cloves
½ square (½ ounce) unsweetened
  chocolate
1½ cups water

1 chicken bouillon cube

1. Wash, drain and dry ducklings; sprinkle with salt.
2. Place duckling pieces, skin-side up, on rack in shallow roasting pan. Bake in preheated 350° F. oven until meat is tender and skin is brown and crisp, about 2 hours. Turn pieces several times during roasting, ending with skin-side up.
3. Cook onion and garlic in oil until tender but not brown.
4. Combine onion mixture, tomato sauce, raisins, peanut butter, sugar, chili powder, cinnamon, cloves, chocolate, water and bouillon cube in blender container. Blend until smooth.
5. Return mixture to saucepan; simmer 15 to 20 minutes, stirring frequently.
6. Pour sauce over duckling at serving time.

# Roast Duckling with Apple & Prune Stuffing, Brown Sauce & Braised Red Cabbage

Serves 4

2 ducklings, weighing 3½ pounds each
3 cooking apples
24 stewed prunes, pitted
salt
corn oil
⅓ cup carrots, sliced

⅓ cup onion, peeled and sliced
⅓ cup celery, sliced
pinch thyme
1 small bay leaf
6 whole peppercorns
Brown Sauce
Braised Red Cabbage

1. Rinse ducklings and pat dry.
2. Peel, core and slice apples. Mix with prunes; add salt to taste.
3. Stuff ducklings with fruit mixture. Truss and tie with string; rub with oil.
4. Place ducklings on rack in roasting pan. Roast, uncovered, in preheated 350° F. oven 2½ hours, turn and roast 15 minutes longer.
5. Add carrots, onion, celery, thyme, bay leaf and peppercorns; roast 20 minutes longer.
6. Remove ducklings to heated platter.
7. Discard vegetables, keeping liquid in pan intact to make Brown Sauce. Skim off about ⅓ cup fat from pan liquid; reserve for use in Braised Red Cabbage.
8. Serve ½ duckling with Brown Sauce and Braised Red Cabbage on the side.

## Brown Sauce

pan drippings from roast ducklings
4 cups stock
2½ tablespoons butter

2½ tablespoons flour
salt to taste
pepper to taste

1. Skim all fat from roasting pan; scrape up brown bits from bottom.
2. Add stock; bring to a boil.
3. Meanwhile, melt butter and stir in flour. Cook and stir until flour mixture is golden brown and smooth.
4. Add flour mixture, a little at a time, to stock mixture until sauce is slightly thickened and of gravy consistency; season with salt and pepper to taste. Strain into gravy boat to serve with or over duckling.

## Braised Red Cabbage

1 medium red cabbage
½ cup applesauce
½ cup sugar
⅓ cup cider vinegar

1 cup water
1 tablespoon currant jelly
⅓ cup reserved fat from roast duckling

1 teaspoon salt

1. Finely shred cabbage and place in heat-proof casserole with lid.
2. Add applesauce, sugar, vinegar, water, currant jelly, duckling fat and salt. Bring to a boil and cover.
3. Transfer to oven and bake in preheated 400° F. oven 2 hours, checking cabbage frequently to prevent drying.

# Duckling with Apple-Pecan Stuffing

Serves 4

2 cleaned ducklings, each weighing
   5 to 6 pounds, cut into serving
   pieces
1 cup dry sherry
½ cup celery, minced
¼ cup onion, minced
1 tablespoon butter or margarine

½ teaspoon poultry seasoning
1 package (8 ounces) seasoned
   stuffing mix
1 cup chicken broth or apple juice
4 cups red apples, chopped
½ cup pecans, chopped
1½ tablespoons cornstarch (optional)

1. Place duckling pieces on rack in roasting pan. Pour sherry over duckling and bake in preheated 350° F. oven 1½ hours, basting often with pan drippings.
2. Meanwhile, cook celery and onion in butter in small skillet until tender. Stir in poultry seasoning.
3. Toss stuffing mix with celery mixture; add broth and toss lightly.
4. Mix in apples and pecans.
5. Remove duckling from pan; reserve drippings.
6. Spread stuffing into 13½ x 9 x 2-inch baking dish. Arrange duckling on top of stuffing. Cover with foil and return to oven. Bake 1 hour longer.
7. To make sauce, if desired, combine drippings skimmed free from fat with enough water to make 1½ cups.
8. Pour into saucepan and stir in cornstarch. Cook and stir over medium heat until thickened.

# Duck Veronique

Serves 2 to 4

1 duckling, weighing 3 to 4 pounds,
   cut in quarters
salt to taste
pepper to taste
1 lemon
1 tablespoon onion, chopped

⅔ cup chicken consommé
1 tablespoon flour
½ cup dry sherry
¼ cup heavy cream
1 cup seedless grapes, pre-cooked
   in boiling water for 2 minutes

1. Sprinkle duckling with salt and pepper; place on rack in shallow roasting pan.
2. Peel lemon and cut into quarters. Scrape white pulp from peel and cut peel into thin strips.
3. Add peel, lemon quarters and chopped onion to consommé; pour over duck.
4. Roast, uncovered, in preheated 325° F. oven 1½ to 2 hours, basting occasionally with pan juices.
5. When duck is done, keep it on a warm dish.
6. Reserve and strain 1½ cups of pan juices.
7. Blend flour and sherry; heat in saucepan with pan juices. Cook, stirring, until thickened.
8. Stir in cream and drained grapes. Pour over duck and keep warm.

# Roast Duck with Orange-Rice Stuffing

Serves 6 to 8

2 cleaned ducklings, weighing
   4½ to 5 pounds each
2 teaspoons salt
¼ teaspoon pepper

Orange Rice Stuffing
¼ cup honey
¼ cup frozen orange juice
   concentrate, thawed and undiluted

1. Sprinkle ducks inside and out with salt and pepper.
2. Spoon 1¾ cups Orange Rice Stuffing into each duck. Do not pack tightly.
3. Skewer neck skin over back. Secure body opening with poultry pins or skewers, or lace with string.
4. Place ducks, breast-side up, on a rack in a shallow open pan. Do not add water, do not cover, do not baste; but do prick ducks often during roasting. Roast in a preheated 325° F. oven 2½ to 3 hours. Duck is well done when drumstick meat is soft when pressed between fingers.
5. Mix together honey and undiluted orange juice concentrate; brush over ducks 30 minutes before end of roasting time.
6. To serve, cut into halves or quarters with poultry shears and sharp knife.

## Orange Rice Stuffing

¼ cup butter or margarine
¼ cup onion, chopped
1 cup water
½ cup orange juice
1 tablespoon orange rind, grated

1 cup celery, chopped
1½ teaspoons salt
¼ teaspoon poultry seasoning
1⅓ cups packed pre-cooked rice
¼ cup parsley, chopped

1. Heat butter in saucepan; add onion and cook until tender, but not brown.
2. Add water, orange juice, orange rind, celery, salt and poultry seasoning. Bring to a boil.
3. Stir in rice. Cover, remove from heat, and let stand 5 minutes.
4. Add parsley and fluff with a fork.

# Roast Duck with Curried Apple Stuffing

Serves 3 to 4

½ cup butter or margarine
1 can (20 ounces) pie-sliced apples, drained
½ cup onion, chopped
¼ cup seedless raisins
3 tablespoons honey
2 tablespoons peanuts, chopped
1½ teaspoons curry powder

1 teaspoon salt
¼ teaspoon pepper
1 cup water
1 package (8 ounces) herb-seasoned stuffing
1 fresh or frozen (thawed) duckling, weighing 5 pounds
Glaze

1. Melt butter in large skillet. Stir in apples, onion, raisins and honey; sauté briefly.
2. Add all remaining ingredients except duck and Glaze, stirring lightly.
3. Rinse duck in cold water and pat dry. Rub inside and out with salt.
4. Stuff lightly; secure with skewers.
5. Place duck, breast-side up, on rack in shallow roasting pan. Roast in preheated 350° F. oven 2 to 2½ hours. (Prick breast of duck with a fork to release fat during roasting.)
6. During last 20 minutes of roasting time, increase heat to 450° F.
7. Pour off fat and continue roasting, brushing frequently with Glaze.
8. To serve, cut in quarters with poultry shears.

## Glaze

Combine ¼ cup honey with 1 teaspoon curry powder.

# Roast Duck à la Phil

Serves 4

## For the Duck

1 cleaned fresh duckling, weighing 4½ to 5 pounds

garlic salt
pepper

1. Cut duckling in quarters; season with garlic salt and pepper.
2. Roast duck on open rack in shallow roasting pan in preheated 400° F. oven 15 minutes to allow excess fat to run off.
3. Reduce oven temperature to 350° F.; roast 2 hours.
4. Drain all fat from pan; pour Orange Sauce over duck.
5. Reheat for 15 minutes before serving. Reserve some sauce to serve at table, if desired.

## Orange Sauce

1 tablespoon cornstarch
1 cup orange juice

⅓ cup sugar
⅓ cup brown sugar

½ teaspoon grated orange rind (optional)

1. Combine all ingredients; stir over low heat until sugar dissolves.
2. Simmer and stir until slightly thick and transparent, about 5 minutes. Extra sauce may be served with duck.

# Barbecued Duck with Apricot Glaze

Serves 4 to 6

2 cleaned ducklings, each
  weighing about 3½ pounds,
  quartered

1 tablespoon salt
½ teaspoon freshly ground black pepper
1 clove garlic, peeled and halved

1 navel orange, scored and cut into vertical halves

1. Season ducks well inside and out with salt and pepper.
2. Rub garlic into skin; prick skin all over with a fork.
3. Place on a rack in roasting pan, breast-side up. Roast in preheated 325° F. oven 1½ hours, or until duck is brown. Turn ducks twice during roasting time, pricking periodically to release fat.
4. Pour off excess fat.

## For the Apricot Glaze

1 orange plus rind (removed in
  strips with a vegetable peeler)
1½ cups apricot preserves
½ cup orange juice
¼ cup water

2 tablespoons red wine vinegar
3 tablespoons Cognac
1 teaspoon salt
watercress or parsley (for
  garnish)

1. With medium slicer of food processor, slice orange, using firm pressure. Wrap in plastic, refrigerate, and reserve for garnish.
2. Place rind and apricot preserves in work bowl, and process with metal blade of processor until mixture is puréed and rind is minced.
3. Add remaining ingredients and process 1 minute.
4. Pour sauce over ducks as soon as removed from oven.
5. Cover and refrigerate ducks in sauce overnight.
6. Remove ducks to a cookie sheet and bring to room temperature.
7. Reserve the marinade. Place ducks on barbecue grill and cook over medium fire, brushing on marinade during cooking. (Watch carefully to prevent marinade from burning.)
8. Duck can also be reheated in 350° F. oven 30 minutes, brushing with marinade. Run under broiler 2 to 3 minutes if more intense color is desired.
9. Cut ducks into serving portions and place on platter. Brush with remaining marinade.
10. Garnish platter with watercress or parsley and reserved orange slices.

# Dove Dinner

Serves 6

12 dressed doves (allow 2 per
 person)
seasoned flour
½ cup butter
1 cup chicken broth
1 cup dry Burgundy
paprika to taste

basil to taste
½ teaspoon celery salt
¼ teaspoon freshly ground
 black pepper
1 cup sliced fresh mushrooms
⅔ cup orange juice, strained
hot cooked wild rice (optional)

1. Split birds in half; dust with seasoned flour.
2. Brown quickly in melted butter in Dutch oven.
3. Mix together broth and wine; pour over birds.
4. Add paprika, basil, celery salt and pepper; bring to a boil.
5. Reduce heat; add mushrooms. Cover and simmer, stirring often, 30 to 35 minutes, or until almost tender.
6. Add orange juice and cook, uncovered, 5 minutes longer.
7. Taste to correct seasonings. Great with hot cooked wild rice.

*NOTE: Dove makes an excellent dish. Most doves respond best to moist heat. Older birds should be casseroled or cooked slowly for a longer period of time to develop the flavor.*

# Southern Roast Wild Duck

Serves 2

1 dressed wild duck
handful fresh mushrooms, sliced
4 tablespoons sweet butter
½ cup wild rice (cooked in
 water 30 minutes according
 to package directions)
2 egg yolks, beaten

½ teaspoon ground sage
½ teaspoon salt
⅛ teaspoon freshly ground black pepper
dash thyme
dash ginger or mace (optional)
1 wild duck liver, broiled and mashed
⅓ cup Port wine

1. Cut off wing tips; set duck aside.
2. Sauté mushrooms in 2 tablespoons butter until golden.
3. Mix sautéed mushrooms with rice, egg yolks, sage, salt, pepper, thyme, ginger and mashed duck liver; stuff duck with mixture.
4. Close opening with skewers or stitching; truss; rub breast generously with butter.
5. Place on rack in roasting pan. Roast, covered, in preheated 475° F. oven, basting often with remaining butter mixed with Port. Cook 25 minutes, or until done.

*NOTE: Wild duck should be roasted very rare. The test of duck done to a turn is that "the blood will follow the knife." To test if duck is done, lift bird and let a few drops run out of the carcass. If blood comes out bluish, it is ready to be served. Duck which is shot in the fall after a summer in the north has a fine-flavored meat. It may be roasted with any stuffing. If shot in the spring, duck may have a strong flavor. Duck with a strong flavor may be soaked 2 to 3 hours in a strong saltwater solution containing 1 tablespoon baking soda.*

# Sautéed Pheasant

### Serves 2 to 3

2 slices bacon, diced
1 cleaned young pheasant, weighing
  2 or 3 pounds, cut in serving pieces
2 onions, peeled and thinly sliced

salt to taste
pepper to taste
1 cup dry white wine
cooked wild rice

1. Sauté bacon; set aside.
2. Sauté pheasant in bacon fat, turning frequently until well browned.
3. Add onions, salt and pepper; add wine.
4. Cover and reduce heat; simmer 30 to 60 minutes.
5. When bird tests tender, serve with pan juices over wild rice.

# Festive Cranberry-Stuffed Pheasant

### Serves 6

3 pheasants, fresh, or thawed if
  frozen
salt
pepper
lemon juice
¼ cup butter or margarine
1 large onion, minced
giblets (optional)

1½ cups fresh or frozen cranberries
1 cup chopped celery
1 package (8 ounces) stuffing mix
½ cup chopped fresh parsley
1 can (10¾ ounces) condensed
  chicken broth
6 strips bacon, halved
½ cup dry white wine

1. Sprinkle pheasant inside and out with salt, pepper and lemon juice.
2. Heat butter in skillet with onion and giblets until onion is golden.
3. Add cranberries and celery; continue cooking 5 minutes longer.
4. Stir in stuffing mix, parsley and chicken broth; blend well.
5. Stuff pheasants; sew or skewer openings.
6. Place pheasants on a rack in a shallow roasting pan. Place strips of bacon on breasts. Roast in preheated 350° F. oven 1½ hours, or until tender, basting several times during roasting with wine. (Any extra stuffing can be placed in a shallow buttered casserole and baked, covered, for last 40 minutes of roasting time.

*NOTE: This is a festive alternative to the usual holiday bird. Serve the birds on a silver platter garnished with parsley or watercress.*

# Broiled Squab

Serves 4

4 cleaned squabs
1 tablespoon baking soda
melted butter
salt to taste

pepper to taste
paprika to taste
4 Trenchers (crusty yeast-raised bread)
minced parsley

1. Clean and split squabs down the back. Wash in water to which about 1 tablespoon baking soda has been added. Rinse and dry well.
2. Place squabs on a rack in a baking pan. Brush generously with melted butter. Broil 4 inches from source of heat 10 to 15 minutes, or until golden.
3. Season with salt, pepper and paprika to taste.
4. Turn and brown second side.
5. Cut Trenchers in half lengthwise, then into slices about the length of the squabs. Hollow out each slice so it will hold the squab.
6. Brush squabs and bread liberally with melted butter; toast in a hot oven until brown.
7. Pour drippings over the top; sprinkle with minced parsley.

# Roast Partridge, Jubilation

Serves 4

4 cleaned young partridges
salt to taste
pepper to taste
8 slices lean bacon
corn oil

water
1 to 2 tablespoons butter
seasoned flour
currant jelly
1 to 2 tablespoons dry Port wine
(optional)

1. Season partridges with salt and pepper.
2. Cover breasts with bacon, tying slices in place with string, or fasten with wooden picks.
3. Brush birds all over with corn oil.
4. Place on sides in heated shallow roasting pan. Roast in preheated 450° F. oven 15 minutes, brushing often with oil.
5. Turn on backs; roast until juice that runs out when bird is lifted and held tail-down is clear without pinkish tinge.
6. Remove birds from oven to warm platter; remove bacon.
7. Add enough water to pan to loosen brown bits on bottom.
8. Meanwhile, soften small amount of flour in cold water and stir into pan juice, stirring to blend.
9. Stir and blend in butter to make smooth paste.
10. Add scant teaspoon currant jelly to sauce, stirring over low heat.
11. Dilute with Port and/or water. Cook, stirring, over low heat until sauce is thickened and smooth.
12. Taste to correct seasonings. Serve gravy spooned over roast partridges.

# Quails Veronique

Serves 6

6 cleaned quails
seasoned flour
½ cup sweet butter
1 cup dry white wine

juice of 1 lemon
1½ cups seedless grapes
½ cup pine nuts
hot wild rice

1. Rub quails with seasoned flour.
2. Melt butter in heavy ovenproof casserole; sauté birds until golden.
3. Add wine and lemon juice; cover and cook over low heat 15 to 20 minutes.
4. Add grapes and pine nuts; cook 10 minutes longer, or until birds are tender.
5. Serve with hot wild rice, spooning sauce over birds and rice.

# Drunken Squabs

Serves 2

3 slices lean bacon
2 cleaned squabs, weighing 1 to
   1¼ pounds each
2 tablespoons flour
1 teaspoon salt
¼ teaspoon freshly ground black
   pepper
1 cup dry red wine (preferably
   Burgundy)

½ cup chicken broth
8 pearl onions, peeled
2 medium carrots, peeled
   and sliced
1 small bay leaf
2 tablespoons minced parsley
2 squab livers, chopped
½ cup sliced fresh mushrooms
hot cooked wild rice (optional)

1. Fry bacon until brown; drain on absorbent paper. Reserve bacon fat in pan.
2. Break bacon into large pieces and place in ovenproof casserole; set aside.
3. Sprinkle each squab with flour seasoned with salt and pepper.
4. Brown squabs quickly in bacon fat; remove birds to casserole.
5. Add remaining seasoned flour to bacon drippings in pan; stir to blend.
6. Add ¾ cup wine and chicken broth; bring to a boil, stirring.
7. Lower heat to simmer and cook 5 minutes, stirring occasionally.
8. Pour wine-broth sauce over squabs in casserole.
9. Add onions and remaining wine to casserole; cover and bake in preheated 325° F. oven 30 minutes.
10. Add carrots, bay leaf, parsley, livers and mushrooms. Cover and bake 40 to 45 minutes longer, or until squabs are tender.
11. Wonderful served over hot cooked wild rice.

NOTE: *If desired, remove squabs to serving platter. Reduce sauce slightly by cooking over direct heat. Add 1 tablespoon currant jelly to sauce, cooking long enough to melt jelly. Taste to correct seasonings. A nice change from the holiday bird for a small family.*

# Roast Stuffed Quail

Serves 6

6 dressed quails
salt
pepper
1 cup Madeira wine
⅓ cup raisins

2 whole cloves
⅔ cup cooked brown rice
pinch ground ginger or mace
1 tablespoon melted butter
additional soft butter

juice of 1 orange

1. Wash and dry birds; sprinkle inside and outside with salt and pepper.
2. Combine Madeira, raisins, and cloves; bring to a boil. Simmer 5 minutes to reduce in volume slightly.
3. Remove cloves; strain mixture, reserving raisins and wine.
4. Combine raisins with rice and ginger; stir in butter.
5. Stuff quails with mixture; truss birds and rub skin with soft butter.
6. Blend reserved wine with orange juice; set aside.
7. Roast quails in preheated 450° F. oven 5 minutes.
8. Reduce oven temperature to 300° F.; roast 25 minutes longer, basting often with wine-orange juice sauce.
9. Arrange birds on heated platters; pour pan juices over all.

# Goose Stuffings
## Fruit Stuffing

Makes enough stuffing for 10- to 12-pound goose

½ cup chopped celery
½ cup chopped onion
¼ cup fat
6 cups day-old bread cubes

2 cups chopped apples
1 cup chopped dried apricots
1 teaspoon salt
½ teaspoon pepper

½ teaspoon thyme

1. Cook celery and onion in fat until tender; pour mixture over bread cubes.
2. Add remaining ingredients and toss lightly to mix well.

## Wild Rice Stuffing

Makes enough for 8- to 10-pound goose

⅔ cup (4 ounces) wild rice
2 cups water
½ teaspoon salt
½ cup finely chopped onions

6 cups day-old white bread
cubes (crusts removed)
1 teaspoon powdered sage
½ teaspoon salt

½ cup melted butter

1. Rinse wild rice thoroughly; bring rice, water and salt to a boil in saucepan.
2. Reduce heat and simmer 30 minutes, or until just tender.
3. Combine onions, bread cubes, sage and salt; mix with cooked wild rice.
4. Add melted butter and toss to mix. Stuff goose lightly; do not pack.

# Curried Turkey Cutlets with Fruit

Serves 6

1½ pounds turkey cutlets
1 teaspoon ground ginger
½ teaspoon garlic powder
⅛ teaspoon ground white pepper
2 tablespoons fresh lemon juice
2 tablespoons flour
2 tablespoons peanut oil
1 cup prunes, pitted
½ cup orange juice

½ cup onion, chopped
1 teaspoon curry powder
1¼ cups chicken broth
2 teaspoons cornstarch
⅛ teaspoon cumin
1 orange, peeled and cut in cart-
   wheel slices
¼ cup unsalted blanched almonds,
   halved and toasted

hot parslied rice (optional)

1. Pound turkey cutlets to flatten slightly.
2. Mix together ½ teaspoon ginger, garlic powder, white pepper and lemon juice; rub on turkey.
3. Dredge cutlets lightly in flour; roll up each piece and secure with wooden pick.
4. Heat oil in skillet and slowly fry turkey rolls until golden.
5. Plump prunes in orange juice about 30 minutes.
6. Sauté onion in turkey drippings until tender; stir in curry powder.
7. Combine broth with cornstarch, remaining ginger and cumin; stir into onion mixture and cook over medium heat until thickened.
8. Place turkey rolls in 2-quart baking dish; add curry sauce. Bake in preheated 350° F. oven 40 minutes.
9. Add prunes, orange slices and almonds; continue baking 10 to 20 minutes, or until turkey is fork-tender.
10. Serve with hot parslied rice, if desired.

# Roast Hen Turkey with German-Style Dressing

Serves 8

1 cleaned hen turkey, weighing 10
   to 12 pounds
salt to taste
pepper to taste
2 bags (6 ounces each) seasoned
   dressing (stuffing) mix

1½ pounds bulk sausage, cooked
   until crumbly (with drippings)
2 or 3 California Pippin apples, peeled
   and diced
1 cup celery, chopped
½ cup onion, chopped

1½ cups water or turkey broth

1. Season turkey with salt and pepper; close body cavities.
2. Place unstuffed turkey, breast-side down, in V-shaped rack in roasting-serving pan. Roast in preheated 325° F. oven 2 to 2½ hours.
3. Meanwhile, combine dressing mix with cooked sausage and drippings, apples, celery, onion and water; toss lightly to blend thoroughly.
4. Remove roasted bird from pan, take out rack and pour off drippings.
5. Place bird, breast-up, in bottom of pan. Spoon dressing around bird.
6. Return turkey to oven. Continue roasting 1 hour longer, or until meat thermometer registers 185° in thigh and dressing is crisp around the edges.

# Roast Turkey with Curried Mushroom Dressing

Serves 4 to 6

1 cleaned fresh turkey, weighing
  5 to 6 pounds
salt

pepper
¼ cup melted butter or margarine
Curried Mushroom Dressing

1. Rub inside turkey with salt and pepper. Tie legs and wings to body with cord.
2. Place bird, breast-side down, on rack in roasting pan. Brush evenly with melted butter.
3. Roast in preheated 325° F. oven 1¾ hours, or until leg meat feels soft when tested with fingers.
4. Let turkey stand 10 minutes before carving.

## Curried Mushroom Dressing

1 bag (6 ounces) seasoned dressing
  (stuffing) mix
½ cup melted butter
¼ cup onion, chopped

¼ cup celery, chopped
½ cup sliced mushrooms
¼ to ½ teaspoon curry powder
¾ cup water

frozen chopped chives (for garnish)

1. Combine all ingredients in mixing bowl; toss thoroughly but lightly.
2. Gently press into greased 1½-quart mold.
3. Bake in preheated 325° F. oven 35 to 40 minutes.
4. Unmold and garnish with chives to serve.

# Turkey Roast with Prune Stuffing

Serves 6 to 8

1 boneless turkey roast, weighing
  3 to 4 pounds
½ cup butter or margarine
1 cup celery, minced

1 bag (6 ounces) cornbread stuffing
1 tablespoon frozen or freeze-dried
  chopped chives
1½ cups plumped California prunes

½ cup liquid from plumped prunes

1. Prepare turkey roast according to package directions.
2. Melt 2 tablespoons butter in skillet. Add celery and cook until transparent.
3. Place cornbread stuffing in a large bowl; add chives and cooked celery.
4. Pit plumped prunes and chop coarsely. Add to dressing mixture with liquid from plumped prunes.
5. Melt remaining butter and pour over dressing mixture. Mix well.
6. Place dressing on double thickness of aluminum foil; wrap.
7. Place dressing in preheated 325° F. oven 1 hour *before* turkey is finished roasting.
8. Remove dressing with turkey roast. Scoop into balls and serve around roast.

# Mushroom-Almond Stuffing

For a 10-pound turkey

¼ cup butter
1 pound mushrooms, sliced
2 cups celery, diced
⅓ cup toasted almonds, slivered
½ cup onion, chopped

5 teaspoons poultry seasoning
¼ teaspoon ground nutmeg
2 quarts bread cubes
3 tablespoons sherry
3 tablespoons water

1. Melt butter in skillet. Sauté mushrooms until golden; push to one side.
2. Add celery; sauté 2 to 3 minutes.
3. Remove pan from heat. Add almonds, onion, poultry seasoning, nutmeg and bread cubes; toss lightly.
4. Sprinkle sherry and water into mixture, tossing lightly.
5. Stuff bird, or bake stuffing separately in greased casserole during last 45 minutes of turkey's roasting time at 300° F.

# Turkey & Dressing, California Style

Serves 8 to 10

12- to 15-pound turkey
salt
freshly ground black pepper
softened butter or margarine, or
    salad oil
2 packages (6 ounces each) 15-minute
    cornbread or chicken-flavor
    stuffing mix

3½ cups water
¾ cup butter or margarine
1 cup chopped onion
1 cup chopped celery
1 cup chopped, peeled tart apple
¼ cup minced fresh parsley

1. Season inside turkey cavity with salt and pepper. Fasten neck skin to back, truss and tie wings and drumsticks to bird.
2. Place turkey, breast-side up, on rack in shallow pan. Brush skin with softened butter.
3. Insert meat thermometer so bulb is in center of inside thigh muscle or thickest part of breast. (Do not allow to touch bone.)
4. For unstuffed turkey, roast, uncovered, in preheated 325° F. oven 4½ to 5 hours (about 180 to 185° F. on meat thermometer).
5. Baste often with pan drippings.
6. About an hour before turkey is done, remove vegetable seasoning packets from stuffing mix. Combine with water and ¼ cup butter in large saucepan. Bring to a simmer; cover and simmer 5 minutes.
7. Meanwhile, sauté onion, celery and apple in remaining butter 10 minutes.
8. Combine mixture with seasoned liquid.
9. Add stuffing crumbs and parsley; mix well.
10. Turn into a buttered 2-quart casserole. Cover and place in oven with turkey; bake 30 minutes, removing cover during last 10 minutes of baking.

# Barbecue Spit-Roasted Stuffed Turkey

### 1 small turkey, weighing 6 to 12 pounds, fresh or frozen and thawed, melted butter or margarine

1. Remove giblets from thawed turkey; wash turkey. Drain and wipe dry with paper towel. (Reserve giblets for stuffing.)
2. Fasten neck skin to back with small skewers. Using heavy cord, tie turkey in four places: tie legs and tail together; tie legs and thighs tightly to body; tie wings in two places to body.
3. Thread one spit prong or fork onto spit, so that points are away from handle. Insert spit into turkey just below breast bone and bring out above the tail. Center turkey on spit.
4. Thread second prong onto spit. Push prong into breast and thigh sections; fasten securely.
5. Tie another cord lengthwise around turkey, wrapping lengthwise cord around each of the crosswise cords.
6. When preparing coals for lightly cooked bird, arrange coals in back half of barbecue. Place a drip pan, about 4 inches longer than turkey, in front half of barbecue. If desired, shape a pan from foil.
7. When coals have reached a medium temperature,* attach spit to motor. Grill until turkey reaches 185° F. internal temperature. (Either insert a meat thermometer in the thickest part of the thigh before starting to grill or use a thermometer that can be inserted periodically for a reading.)
8. The following chart can be used as a guide for barbecuing time:

| Ready-To-Cook Weight | Approximate Cooking Time |
|---|---|
| 6 to 8 pounds | 3 to 3⅓ hours |
| 8 to 10 pounds | 3½ to 4 hours |
| 10 to 12 pounds | 4 to 5 hours |

9. About 1 hour before turkey is done, wrap selected stuffing in foil packet and place on coals. Turn occasionally and cook until heated throughout. (Stuffing may also be done in oven.)
10. Remove turkey from spit and let stand 15 minutes before carving.

## *How To Judge the Temperature of a Charcoal Briquet Fire

Different brands of charcoal give off varying degrees of heat. To test temperature of a charcoal briquet fire, it is recommended that you hold your hand, palm-side down, just above the grill. Judge temperature by number of seconds hand can be kept in position, using the following guide:

| | |
|---|---|
| high or hot . . . . . . . . . . . . . . . . . . . . . . . . . . . . . . . . . . . . . . . . . . . | 2 seconds |
| medium high or hot . . . . . . . . . . . . . . . . . . . . . . . . . . . . . . . . . | 3 seconds |
| medium . . . . . . . . . . . . . . . . . . . . . . . . . . . . . . . . . . . . . . . . . . . . | 4 seconds |
| low . . . . . . . . . . . . . . . . . . . . . . . . . . . . . . . . . . . . . . . . . . . . | 5 seconds |

To lower temperature of charcoal fire, raise grill or separate coals. To raise temperature, tap the outer gray layer from coals and push coals closer together. If more coals are needed, add them to outer edge of hot coals.

# Wild Rice Stuffing (Cooked over Coals)

Makes 3 cups

1 package (6 ounces) long grain and
  wild rice mix
¼ pound pork sausage
1 cup chopped celery

½ cup chopped onion
½ teaspoon thyme leaves
1 teaspoon sage
1 teaspoon salt

¼ teaspoon pepper

1. Prepare rice mix according to package directions; set aside.
2. Break sausage into pieces; brown in small skillet.
3. Remove sausage and pour off all but about 2 tablespoons of drippings from skillet.
4. Sauté celery and onion in drippings until crisp-tender.
5. Combine cooked rice, sausage, sautéed vegetables and remaining ingredients in mixing bowl.
6. Turn onto foil, wrap, and place on coals.
7. Cook 1 hour, turning occasionally, or bake in covered casserole in preheated 350° F. oven 30 minutes, or until heated through.

# Roast Turkey with Fig-Stuffing Muffins

Serves 12

2 bags (6 ounces each) cornbread stuffing
½ cup melted butter or margarine
3 eggs, well beaten

1½ cups chicken broth
½ cup crisp bacon, crumbled
1½ cups dried figs, chopped

12 whole figs

1. Mix together stuffing, melted butter, eggs, chicken broth, bacon and chopped figs in a bowl.
2. Spoon mixture into 12 greased muffin cups. Top each muffin with a whole fig. Bake in a preheated 350° F. oven 30 to 35 minutes, or until firm. (Cover muffins with foil if figs brown too quickly.)
3. Unmold and serve with your roast turkey.
4. These muffins can be made ahead of time and baked. When ready to use, cover with foil and bake in preheated 350° F. oven 15 minutes.
5. These muffins can also be frozen. When ready to use, unwrap and heat, covered lightly, in preheated 350° F. oven 30 to 35 minutes.
6. These muffins can also be microwaved. Spoon mixture into 12 greased custard cups; arrange cups 6 at a time, in a circle in microwave oven. Microwave on HIGH 4 to 5 minutes.
7. Frozen muffins can be reheated in a microwave, heating them on HIGH 2 to 3 minutes, then allowing them to stand for 2 minutes to allow heat to distribute.

NOTE: An interesting alternative to stuffing.

# Cornbread Stuffing

Makes 2 quarts dressing (for an 8-pound turkey)

1 package (15 ounces) cornbread mix
1½ cups chopped celery
1 cup chopped onion
½ cup pitted ripe olives,
    quartered

½ cup butter or margarine
1 teaspoon powdered thyme
½ teaspoon seasoned salt
½ cup chopped pecans
¾ cup chicken broth

1. Prepare and bake cornbread mix according to package directions.
2. Cool and coarsely crumble into a large bowl or kettle. Set aside.
3. Sauté celery, onion and olives in butter; add thyme, seasoned salt and pecans.
4. Add sautéed mixture to cornbread mix, tossing lightly.
5. Add chicken broth, mixing until moistened.
6. Turn mixture into a buttered 2½-quart casserole or baking dish.
7. Cover and bake in preheated 350° F. oven 25 minutes.
8. Uncover and bake 10 minutes longer.

NOTE: Double the recipe to stuff a 16-pound turkey.

# Roast Turkey, Southern Style

Serves 8 to 10

1 cup cooked ham, diced
1 cup onion, chopped
1 teaspoon poultry seasoning
½ teaspoon sage
2 tablespoons butter or margarine
2 cans (10½ ounces each) chicken or
    chicken giblet gravy

4 cups dry bread cubes
2 cups coarse cornbread crumbs
1 egg, slightly beaten
½ cup raisins
cleaned, dressed turkey, weighing
    10 pounds

1. Brown ham, onion, poultry seasoning and sage in butter in saucepan until onion is tender.
2. Add ½ cup gravy.
3. Toss lightly with bread cubes, cornbread crumbs, egg and raisins.
4. Fill body and neck cavities of turkey with stuffing; secure with skewers. Fasten legs by tying with string. Tuck wings behind shoulders.
5. Place in roasting pan and cover loosely with foil. Roast in preheated 325°F. oven 4 hours, allowing 25 minutes per pound or until internal temperature reaches 185° F. and leg moves easily.
6. Uncover during last hour to brown, basting occasionally.
7. Remove turkey from pan. Spoon off fat, saving 6 tablespoons drippings.
8. On top of range, in roasting pan, combine remaining gravy and drippings. Heat, stirring to loosen browned bits. Serve with turkey and stuffing.

# Roast Halved Turkey à l'Orange

Serves 6 to 8

1 half-bodied turkey, weighing
   5 to 6 pounds
salt
pepper
2 tablespoons butter or margarine, melted

½ cup brown sugar, packed
¼ cup honey
¼ cup fresh orange juice
1 teaspoon orange peel, grated
   or cut in julienne strips

1. Rinse turkey; drain and pat dry. Rub salt and pepper into body cavity.
2. Tie leg to tail with string. Lay wing flat over white meat; tie string around breast to hold wing down. Skewer skin to meat along cut edges to prevent shrinking.
3. Place turkey on rack in shallow roasting pan, skin-side up. Brush skin with melted butter.
4. Insert meat thermometer into inside thigh muscle, not touching bone. Roast in preheated 325° F. oven 2 to 2½ hours, or until meat thermometer registers 180° to 185° F.
5. Combine brown sugar, honey, orange juice and orange peel in small saucepan. Heat until brown sugar dissolves, stirring constantly.
6. Brush glaze over turkey during last hour of roasting, basting often to use all of glaze.
7. When turkey is done, remove from oven and let stand 20 minutes before carving.

# Clay-Cooked Turkey Breast

Serves 3 or 4

1 half turkey breast, weighing
   2½ to 3 pounds
salt
1 cup onion, chopped
1 cup carrots, chopped
1 cup celery, chopped
1 cup mushrooms, sliced

¼ cup parsley, minced
1 teaspoon thyme
½ teaspoon poultry seasoning
⅛ teaspoon pepper
½ cup chicken broth
⅓ cup melted margarine
cornstarch

1. Submerge clay cooker in water for 15 minutes (or as directed).
2. Rub turkey breast with salt.
3. Mix together onion, carrots, celery, mushrooms and parsley.
4. Toss with thyme, poultry seasoning, ½ teaspoon salt and pepper.
5. Place, breast-side up, in clay cooker; pour vegetables over and around.
6. Mix together broth and melted margarine; pour over breast and vegetables.
7. Cover and place in cold oven. Bake at 450° F. 1 to 1½ hours, or until meat is tender or registers 170° to 175° F. with a meat thermometer in the thickest part. Baste once or twice during baking.
8. Remove breast; let sit 4 to 5 minutes, then slice.
9. Thicken pan juices with a little cornstarch mixed with water; pour over turkey slices.

# Pot-of-Gold Turkey Dinner

Serves 3 to 4

1 turkey half-breast,
weighing 2 to 2½ pounds
¼ pound butter or margarine
3 tablespoons flour
1 teaspoon sugar
½ teaspoon salt
⅛ teaspoon cinnamon
1½ cups orange juice

1 teaspoon fresh lemon juice
1 tablespoon sherry
½ cup slivered almonds
½ cup raisins
1 can (8 ounces) crushed pineapple,
undrained
1 can (16 ounces) sweet potatoes,
drained

1. Rinse turkey half-breast; pat dry.
2. Brown turkey on both sides in butter. Remove turkey and set aside.
3. Combine flour, sugar, salt and cinnamon; blend into pan juices, cooking 1 to 2 minutes.
4. Combine orange juice, lemon juice and sherry; gradually stir into pan, keeping mixture smooth.
5. Add almonds and raisins.
6. Return turkey to pan; cover and simmer 1 hour.
7. Add pineapple and sweet potatoes; cover and simmer 15 minutes.
8. Remove turkey breast and slice. Serve with sweet potatoes and sauce.

NOTE: A wonderful way to prepare a holiday meal, all-in-one, for a small family.

# Roast Half-Breast of Turkey with Mushrooms

Serves 4 to 6

1 half-breast of turkey (about
2¼ to 2½ pounds)
5 tablespoons melted butter
½ teaspoon salt
½ teaspoon paprika

½ teaspoon tarragon, crumbled
⅛ teaspoon white pepper
½ cup dry white table wine
1 cup sliced fresh mushrooms,
or 1 can (2 ounces) drained

1 package (6 ounces) dry stuffing mix

1. Place turkey breast in shallow baking pan.
2. Melt 2 tablespoons butter; add salt, paprika, tarragon and white pepper.
3. Spoon butter mixture over turkey breast.
4. Bake in preheated 450° F. oven 10 minutes.
5. Combine wine and mushrooms; pour over turkey.
6. Reset oven thermostat to 325° F.; bake 1 hour longer, basting once or twice with pan drippings.
7. Remove from oven and transfer to heated serving platter; keep warm. Reserve pan drippings.
8. Prepare stuffing mix according to package instructions, using drained drippings for part of liquid. Add remaining butter.

# Elegant Turkey Cutlets with Grape Sauce

Serves 6 to 8

6 to 8 turkey cutlets
seasoned salt
lemon pepper
¼ cup melted butter
1 clove garlic, pressed
⅓ cup minced onion
2 tablespoons flour

1 chicken bouillon cube
1 cup water
3 tablespoons vinegar
¼ cup prepared yellow mustard
¼ cup honey
2 cups halved, seeded grapes
minced parsley

hot cooked rice (optional)

1. Season turkey cutlets generously with seasoned salt and lemon pepper.
2. Brown cutlets in 2 tablespoons butter in skillet; remove and set aside in warm place.
3. Add remaining butter to skillet; sauté garlic and onion until tender.
4. Add flour and crushed bouillon cube; cook about 1½ minutes.
5. Stir in water, vinegar and mustard. Cook, stirring, over low heat until thickened.
6. Stir in honey; fold in grapes. Cook several minutes.
7. Pour sauce over turkey, arranged on serving platter. Sprinkle with minced parsley. Serve alone or with hot cooked rice.

# Stuffed Turkey Thigh

Serves 2

1 small onion, peeled and chopped
1 stalk celery with leaves, chopped
1 clove garlic, peeled and chopped
2 tablespoons corn oil
1 small apple, peeled, cored and thinly
  sliced
8 sprigs parsley, chopped
6 mushrooms, chopped

½ teaspoon sage
½ teaspoon thyme
½ teaspoon salt
¼ teaspoon basil
¼ teaspoon ground white pepper
1 cup toasted stale bread, cut
  into croutons
3½ cups apple juice

1 turkey thigh, weighing 1½ pounds

1. Sauté onion, celery and garlic in corn oil until softened.
2. Add apple, parsley, mushrooms, sage, thyme, salt, basil and pepper. Stir to mix well.
3. Add croutons and apple juice; mix well.
4. Lay turkey thigh, skin-side down, on cutting board. Cut a slit with sharp paring knife through turkey meat to bone; carefully remove bone.
5. Make a horizontal cut in each side of bone cavity to open or "butterfly" thigh.
6. Place ¾ cup stuffing in cavity. Close by sewing or looping a string around thigh several times. (Thigh should look balloon-shaped.)
7. Mound remaining stuffing in greased 8-inch cake pan or casserole.
8. Place stuffed thigh directly on top of dressing. Cover loosely with aluminum foil and roast in preheated 350° F. oven 30 minutes.
9. Remove foil, continue roasting 45 minutes longer, or until juices run clear when skin is pierced.

# Roast Turkey Half-Breast

Serves 4

1 turkey half-breast, weighing
2 to 2½ pounds

salt
freshly ground black pepper

1. Rinse turkey half-breast; pat-dry. Rub both sides with salt and pepper.
2. Place turkey on rack in roasting pan, skin-side up. Insert meat thermometer into thickest part, making certain it does not touch bone.
3. Roast in preheated 350° F. oven 1¾ to 2 hours, or until meat thermometer registers 180° to 185° F.

*NOTE: A good buy for a small household. If desired, turkey can be spread with cranberry sauce during last 30 minutes of roasting to form a glaze.*

# Barbecued Turkey Steaks I

Serves 4

3 tablespoons vinegar
2 tablespoons dry sherry
¼ cup vegetable oil
2 tablespoons catsup
1 tablespoon parsley, chopped

¾ teaspoon onion salt
¼ teaspoon savory, crushed
¼ teaspoon dill weed
⅛ teaspoon garlic powder
⅛ teaspoon pepper

1 pound turkey steaks or breast slices

1. Combine vinegar, sherry, oil, 1 tablespoon catsup, parsley, onion salt, savory, dill weed, garlic powder and pepper. Pour over turkey steaks in shallow pan.
2. Cover and refrigerate pan, turning occasionally. Marinate several hours.
3. Drain steaks well.
4. Stir remaining catsup into marinade.
5. Grill steaks over hot coals, 4 to 6 minutes, depending on thickness. Brush steaks when turned with reserved marinade. Serve piping hot.

# Barbecued Turkey Steaks II

Serves 6

6 turkey steaks
1 cup lemon-lime carbonated
beverage

½ cup salad oil
½ cup soy sauce
⅛ teaspoon garlic powder

1. Buy turkey steaks or cut your own.
2. Combine remaining ingredients; marinate steaks 4 to 24 hours, turning several times.
3. Cook over medium coals 15 to 20 minutes, or until meat is done, brushing with marinade occasionally during cooking.

# Turkey Ham Loaf with Mustard Sauce

Serves 6 to 8

½ cup soda cracker crumbs
½ cup milk
1 egg, beaten
2 tablespoons onion, chopped
¼ teaspoon pepper
1 pound ground turkey ham

1 pound ground pork
¼ cup water
¼ cup vinegar
½ cup brown sugar, packed
½ teaspoon dry mustard
Mustard Sauce

1. Soak cracker crumbs in mixture of milk, egg, onion and pepper.
2. Combine mixture with ground turkey ham and pork.
3. Pack into greased 9 x 5-inch loaf pan.
4. Combine water, vinegar, brown sugar and mustard; pour over loaf.
5. Bake in preheated 350° F. oven 1 hour.
6. Let stand 10 to 15 minutes before slicing. Serve with Mustard Sauce.

## Mustard Sauce

Makes about 1½ cups

¼ cup sugar
1 tablespoon flour
2 teaspoons dry mustard

1 cup half-and-half
1 egg yolk
¼ cup vinegar

1. Combine sugar, flour and mustard in saucepan.
2. Mix together half-and-half and egg; gradually add to dry ingredients.
3. Cook and stir over low heat until thickened.
4. Gradually stir in vinegar. Serve warm.

# Turkey Spaghetti Sauce

Serves 6

2 medium onions, peeled and minced
2 garlic cloves, peeled and minced
¼ cup olive oil
½ cup celery, minced
¼ pound cleaned fresh mushrooms, sliced
3½ cups (one 28-ounce can) tomatoes

1 can (6 ounces) tomato paste
2 teaspoons salt
⅛ teaspoon cayenne pepper
1 teaspoon sugar
½ teaspoon basil
1 bay leaf
1 cup turkey pan juices
1 cup water

1. Lightly sauté onions and garlic in olive oil in large saucepan.
2. Add celery and mushrooms; brown.
3. Add remaining ingredients, bring to a boil, then lower to simmer.
4. Cook, at simmer, uncovered, about 1 hour. (Makes enough sauce for 1 pound cooked spaghetti.)

NOTE: Sauce can be made with one cup of broth or white wine instead of turkey juices, if desired.

# Curried Turkey over Broiled Bananas

### Serves 4

2 tablespoons butter or margarine
½ cup chopped onion
1 cup chopped celery
3 tablespoons flour
¾ teaspoon salt
½ teaspoon curry powder

1 chicken bouillon cube, crushed
1½ cups milk
2 cups cut-up cooked turkey
½ cup sliced pitted ripe olives
Broiled Bananas

1. Melt butter in saucepan.
2. Add onion and celery; cook over medium heat until tender.
3. Blend in flour, salt, curry powder and crushed bouillon cube; cook 1 to 2 minutes, stirring constantly.
4. Gradually stir in milk; cook constantly until mixture thickens and comes to a boil. Simmer 2 to 3 minutes.
5. Add turkey and olives; heat through. Serve over Broiled Bananas.

## Broiled Bananas

4 bananas

melted butter

1. Cut 4 bananas in half lengthwise.
2. Place in a buttered baking dish; brush with melted butter.
3. Broil 3 to 5 minutes, or until golden brown.

# Turkey Delight

### Serves 6

3 cups cooked rice
1½ cups dairy sour cream
1 teaspoon powdered mustard
1 can (11 ounces) condensed Cheddar cheese soup
½ teaspoon salt
⅛ teaspoon ground black pepper
½ cup pitted ripe olives, sliced

1 can (4 ounces) sliced mushrooms, drained
1½ cups smoked turkey, cut in julienne strips
¾ cup dry roasted cashew nuts or peanuts, coarsely chopped
¾ cup crushed round butter crackers
1 tablespoon chopped parsley

1. Combine rice, sour cream, mustard, soup, salt and pepper; mix well.
2. Stir in olives, mushrooms, and turkey; add ½ cup cashews.
3. Turn into a shallow greased 2-quart baking dish. Cover and bake in preheated 350° F. oven 20 to 25 minutes.
4. Meanwhile, combine remaining cashews, cracker crumbs and parsley; uncover casserole and sprinkle on top.
5. Bake 10 minutes longer. Serve piping hot.

NOTE: Casserole works well made with leftover cooked chicken, ham or duck.